D0358675

Make Your Mind Up

Make Your Mind Up

My Guide to Finding Your Own
Style, Life, and Motavation!

BETHANY MOTA

CENTURY

CENTURY

1 3 5 7 9 10 8 6 4 2

Century
20 Vauxhall Bridge Road
London SW1V 2SA

Century is part of the Penguin Random House group of companies whose addresses
can be found at global.penguinrandomhouse.com

Copyright © 2017 by Bethany Mota

Bethany Mota has asserted her right under
the Copyright, Designs and Patents Act, 1988, to be identified as the
author of this work.

First published in the United Kingdom in 2017 by Century

www.penguin.co.uk

A CIP catalogue record for this book is available from the British Library.

ISBN 9781780896502

Interior design by Jason Snyder

Printed and bound in Germany by Firmengruppe APPL, aprinta druck, Wemding

Penguin Random House is committed to a sustainable future for our business,
our readers and our planet. This book is made from Forest Stewardship
Council® certified paper.

To my viewers,
this is for you

Contents

HEY, GUYS!   *viii*

INTRODUCTION   *xi*

Getting MOTAVATED 1

How I follow my passions, find my confidence, and feed my creativity

1 CONFIDENCE   2

2 CREATIVITY   32

Getting HEALTHY 47

How I keep my body strong through food and fitness

3 FOOD   48

4 FITNESS   66

Getting GORGEOUS 89

How I play up my personal clothing and makeup style

5 STYLE   90

6 BEAUTY   106

Getting SOCIAL 125

How I find and build relationships through friends and dating

7 FRIENDS   126

8 DATING   142

Getting CHILL 163

How I feed my soul with alone time and a happy home

9 ME TIME   164

10 HOME   180

THANK YOU!   207

ACKNOWLEDGMENTS   209

Hey, guys!

I'm so glad you're here, because I would love to tell you a story. It's about how when I was little, I didn't have a voice.

What I mean by that is that I was so shy and scared to speak up, some people thought I was mute. Like, literally. They thought I was unable to talk. Around my sister or my parents, I was chatty, loud, and always said exactly what was on my mind, but I never opened up to people outside of my family. In any crowded situation, I would hide behind my mom and I wouldn't say a word.

Since then, a *ton* of things have happened—both big and small—to get me where I am today. I've finally found my voice, and now I get to share my ideas in ways I only dreamed of as a child. But the only way I got here was by making my mind up about who I wanted to be. Then, I used sheer motivation by overcoming some difficult experiences, facing my fears, and putting my authentic self out there. Now I want to share my story and hopefully inspire you to live the life you want to live, say the things you want to say, and be the person you want to be.

I would never tell someone how to live his or her life, because there isn't just one way to live creatively, stylishly, beautifully, or confidently. But I would love to take you guys on a tour of how I live mine.

Want to come along?

XO,
Bethany

INTRODUCTION

Messy Little Me

You wouldn't know it by looking at my style now that I post on my Insta feed, but I was a total tomboy as a kid. I'd wear a tank top and little shorts, and my hair was a really short bob with choppy bangs my mom cut for me herself. Most of the time, I was running around outdoors, so my hair was usually a hot mess and I was *always* dirty. But my parents just let me do my own thing, which I'm eternally grateful for. Because even though I've cut down on running around outdoors in the dirt, I'm still messy in my own way. And the freedom my parents gave me in those early years encouraged me to follow my own unique path. Which is exactly how I got to where I am today.

I grew up in a town called Los Banos, outside of San Francisco, with my mom, Tammy, my dad, Tony, and my sister, Brittany, who is five years older than me. People often ask if Brittany and I got along or if she ever picked on me, but the truth is that I was the one who was mean to her! It's actually a joke in my family because our relationship was the *opposite* of the older sibling picking on the younger sister. As a little tot, I would pull her hair and wrestle her to the floor—and being the accommodating, sweet big sister she was, she could see I was having fun and so she just dealt with it. I only teased (okay, tormented) her for a couple of years, but I still feel so bad about it. Now, of course, we're the closest of friends. She's married and has a daughter, Marin Mae (the cutest, most lovable niece a girl could ask for), and we talk or FaceTime every day.

When I was five, we moved into another house in the same town, but this one was on a dairy farm. There were only about five houses on the property, so it felt a little isolated. Most neighbors were married couples without kids, so my sister and I didn't have a lot of options for playmates. You know how some kids play with neighborhood kids growing up? Me, I made friends with . . . cows. I'm not kidding; there were cows in pens *everywhere*. They were just so cute that I'd try and take ownership over each cow by petting and naming them. Granted, at five years old I was teeny and they were huge, but I wasn't scared of them like I was of people. Go figure.

I remember one morning, I woke up to see the cows had escaped their pen and were surrounding our house. When I looked out my bedroom window, there were three cows just chilling, staring at me through the glass. It was really bizarre. And I've always wondered how the cows got out, because someone would have to *let* them out, right? And how long had they been watching me sleep? Okay, I'm getting off track. *Focus*, Beth.

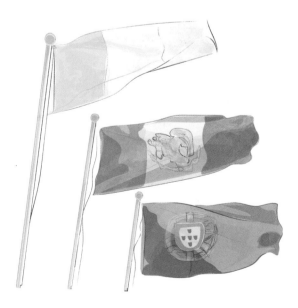

I'll never forget how one summer a family finally moved in with kids my sister's and my age. "Welp," I thought, "I guess these kids will be our friends." I was quiet around them at first—the way I always was around new people—but the more time our families spent together, the more my neighbors became like family. Those kids became my first real, live friends.

There was a trail behind my house that the four of us (my neighbors, my sister, and I) would explore, which was scary and full of snakes (in retrospect: not the best idea). We also had one of those home jungle gyms in my backyard. Playing outside and letting my imagination run wild was my paradise. I could make an entire imaginary world out of sticks and stones, and I absolutely loved it.

When I wasn't exploring the great out-doors, making friends with cows, or crossing paths with scary snakes, my family and I would drive to Portuguese *festa*s. (My dad is from Portugal, and my mom is Mexican and Irish.) There was a big Portuguese community in Los Banos, and every month or so, we'd all gather at the community center for a *festa* to share Portuguese music and food. We'd sit at tables on the ground floor, serving ourselves from pots of food on each table; later, everyone would go upstairs and dance until 1 am. There were partner dances and group dances with a lot of twirling involved, and I was always dancing along—but I'm pretty sure I wasn't doing any of it right! I was proud to be a part of that community, which felt like a big, extended family. It also brought me much closer to my dad's family—especially my grandma and grandpa. Both of them only spoke Portuguese, but I always felt very connected to them having shared those experiences.

I was an expert at entertaining myself at home alone, too. Since iPads were obviously a thing of the distant future at the time, I had a lot of toys that I kept myself occupied with when I wasn't running wild or spending time with my family: baby dolls, Barbies, the classic Fisher-Price car that you climbed into, and a life-sized kitchen set with all the fake pots that I played with in my cooking phase. I still smile when I think of my fun and free childhood, because I wouldn't have wanted to grow up any other way.

WHAT I WANTED TO BE WHEN I GREW UP

When I was really young, what I wanted to be when I grew up changed all the time. My first dream was that I would work as a waitress at an old-fashioned diner—but only if I could ride around on roller skates while giving people their milkshakes. I'm not kidding, it was a serious dream of mine! I often thought about how I could get that job. I just liked the vibe of it, rolling around on my skates and making people happy.

Then, I wanted to be an accountant for a while, but that was a short-lived fantasy that ended when I found out what an accountant was.

I also wanted to be a fashion designer. You know when you used to play dress up? Well, in my version of that game I was a fashion designer and I "designed" all the clothes I was wearing. I loved the idea of making a conceptual idea into a reality, and that love of creativity plays a pretty significant role in my career now. And so, looking back on my childhood, it's pretty funny that my favorite subject in school was science—especially the chemistry experiments. Although, who knows, maybe that was the beginning of my passion for experimenting with DIY projects.

Even though my ideas for what I wanted to be growing up kept changing, I knew one thing for sure: I wanted it to be different. I felt like I was destined to do something unexpected in life . . . but I just didn't know what.

Keeping It Moving

We finally got a family computer when I was seven years old. At first, it didn't have Internet, so we'd insert CDs to play dress-up games and Pet Shop. And then, of course, I had Hit Clips on a little key chain that I toted around with me at all times. It was this really tiny MP3 player that played songs off of these chunky memory cards. I remember I bought a Britney Spears Hit Clip—and I don't even think those memory cards stored the full song, to be honest. I think it was like a minute, right? Compared to iPhones, it's pathetic, but hey—at the time they seemed so awesome. I would listen to Britney, *NSYNC, and Backstreet Boys, and I'd steal my sister's clips because she had more than I did. Walking around the playground, jamming out to Hit Clips, was *definitely* a thing. I thought I was so cool.

When I was eight, we moved out of Los Banos to a town called Dos Palos; and three years later, we moved back to Los Banos to a different house than the one we'd started in. What's funny is that, even though we didn't move far each time, I always thought moving a lot was normal because it's all I knew. I had childhood friends who grew up their entire lives in the same home, but I was used to moving every few years. We also took a lot of family road trips up and down California, and I think changing neighborhoods and visiting different cities made me more open-minded. The way I saw it, if my state was that big, my country was even bigger, which meant the world was huge! Getting those small tastes of different places, even if only separated by a few miles, made me determined to see what else was out there.

Up until I was eight years old, my mom homeschooled both my sister and me. But when I reached third grade—just after we moved to Dos Palos—Brittany really wanted to go to public school to see what it was all about. I was given the choice, too, and because I was obsessed with copying everything my big sister did (that is, when she'd let me!) our parents sent us both to public school for the first time.

There I was, an awkward little kid—who, by the way, had just started wearing glasses for the very first time—starting school in the middle of the school year, among kids who'd been going to school together for years. Talk about feeling out of place! So yeah, I was petrified. My first day was overwhelming, to say the least. (I'm still eternally grateful for the little girl who talked to me that day, so I didn't have to eat lunch completely alone.) Most days after that, I kept to myself, trying to learn the ropes by watching everyone. But I struggled that first year of public school, especially with my studies. I wasn't used to normal classroom activities like speaking up in class or doing group projects. And because I was so used to doing work at my own pace at home, I found it hard to focus with distractions I wasn't used to, like friends, acne, and boys. I only made two friends in school that first year.

Still, the experience helped break me out of my shell. Three years later, I took it even further when, in sixth grade, I tried

cheerleading. I was a Pomerette, which meant the routines were all very dance-inspired, which I loved. We cheered at the Friday night football games. Every time I put on my cheer uniform, I felt a subtle but definitely noticeable shift; suddenly, I was a performer who had a job to do, so the second I stepped into the middle of that field for our dance, I left my insecurities behind and gave it my all.

Painfully Shy

When I say I was shy, by the way? Well, I was *really* shy. I'll never forget when I was around ten and my sister had her friends over. I was in the living room with them but I wasn't talking. (Quick shout out to Brittany here, though: Thanks for letting your little sis hang out with you! Well, at least *near* you.) I just sat there not saying anything because I was scared of saying the wrong thing—something they wouldn't find cool or interesting or funny. Then, I finally said something and one of them goes, "Oh my gosh! I didn't know Bethany speaks!" I'm serious; people thought I was mute.

My sister was the exact opposite. She's always been really talkative. She played all the sports and had all the friends, so anyone who met us at the same time automatically labeled her as "the outgoing one" and me as "the shy one." And because of that, I labeled myself: "Oh, right, *I'm* the shy one."

What I've learned is that people have a need for certainty; they want to know how to define not only things, but people, too. So once I was certain I was shy, that became my safe place and I just stuck with it. I've talked about this with a few other formerly shy people, and they all say the same thing: once you're labeled as shy, it's easier to just fit that mold instead of trying to break it. That said, easier doesn't mean better. In many moments, I stayed quiet when I wanted to speak, kept my hand in my lap even when I knew the answer, and stuck to my quiet-as-a-mouse MO—even if I was missing out on something fun.

As I got older, being shut in that "shy" box started bothering me. So I began to ask myself why I was shy to begin with. Why I shut up in social situations. Why I was afraid of putting myself out there. And once I started asking myself those questions, I realized my biggest fear was that someone would think I was stupid, and so I felt like it was safer to not say anything than to say the wrong thing.

But I didn't like how much I was isolating myself, so I came up with a plan: I decided I would *make* myself more outgoing. From then on, when my sister's friends came over, I would look at the most outgoing person in the room and try to match his or her energy. If I was louder and more fun, they would have to like me, right?

But it wasn't working; I wasn't fitting in *or* feeling better about myself. So then I started wondering why. After all, I was being the most outgoing one in the room, so I should be happier, right? Wrong. Even though I talked the loudest, laughed the hardest, or told the most jokes, nothing had really changed because I was forcing it. And the more I pretended to be someone I wasn't, the more drained I felt. Faking it was exhausting! While I was trying to show the funny side of myself, I wasn't expressing that side in the most authentic, Bethany way possible. I felt like I was putting on a show, or playing a role, and my heart wasn't in it. I wanted to be me—the silly, real, goofy, natural me—more than anything. I just needed to figure out how.

RANDOM ME FACT: I'M A LEFTIE

Yep, I'm a leftie, and boy did I hate it growing up. My family and most of the kids in school were all right-handed, so I hated being different. But there were other annoying things about it—and all the lefties out there will know what I'm talking about. When you write as a leftie, it's more complicated, because you always smear whatever you just wrote, so I grew up always having inky blue pen smudges or metallic gray pencil marks on the side of my hand (and I have iffy handwriting to begin with, so combine the two and you get a handwritten disaster). And if I ever had to sit close beside someone who was a rightie? Forget it. We were constantly bumping elbows, which—hello!—is super-awkward. So over the years, I started using my right hand for as many things as possible, but when it comes to my writing, I'm still as leftie as it gets—and I have lots of terrible, smeared pieces of notebook paper to show for it.

Bullied by My Peers

One day, when I was eleven, I turned on the family computer and went to MySpace, and that's when I saw an unfamiliar page titled "Bethany Mota." I remember thinking, "That's not the profile picture I uploaded a few days ago." The photo didn't match, because it wasn't my page; someone had made a fake MySpace pretending to be me. They'd taken a bunch of my own photos from my real page and posted them to this fake one, with really mean captions about my weight and physical appearance.

One photo said, "Look at me, I'm so fat in this photo." Another said, "Look at how ugly my face looks in this one." In that moment, I just froze. My heart pounded and my mind raced and I finally knew what people meant about breaking into a cold sweat. It was so surreal; I couldn't believe it was happening. I didn't even know how to process it at first because I was having such an intense mix of emotions about it, from shock to anger to total confusion. But blanketing it all in that moment was one overwhelming feeling: sadness. These were pictures I loved, and someone had stolen them from me, changing the happy meanings and memories to cruel ones.

I didn't know what to do. So I just stepped away from the computer and went to my room. I didn't want to talk about it; I didn't want to even acknowledge that it was real. I also didn't know who was behind the fake profile at that point. I was too busy wondering why someone would do something like this to me. I had always treated people with kindness—and I only talked to two people at school anyway!

I tried to act like the page didn't exist and just shut myself in my room for a while. But every few hours, I would go back to the family computer and visit it—desperate to see if the person behind the page had taken it down, or updated it. Over time, the bullies added more photos and mean captions. Eventually they abandoned the page and stopped updating it, but they didn't remove it. I knew the world wasn't actively looking for it, but still: that fake profile was up there for anyone I knew to see.

I finally told my mom about it and she and my family tried to comfort me, but they couldn't fix my feelings. So I told people I was fine. But I wasn't; I wasn't fine at all. Because whoever made that page about me had ripped a hole in how I felt about myself. Up until that point, I had never thought about physical appearance. But now I couldn't help but overanalyze everything they posted. I found it hard to differentiate my truth from the harsh words on MySpace. I started to wonder: *Am I fat? Am I ugly?* For the first time in my life, I began to contemplate my weight and wonder if I *needed* makeup. Until those bullies broke through, I never thought about any of these things, but the site made me self-conscious about every aspect of my appearance, from the style of my hair to the polish on my toes.

At the time, it felt like my world was crashing down. I wasn't sure if being myself was good enough anymore. Eventually, the painful experience of that day and those that followed would come to shape me and help me become a stronger person—I just didn't know it yet.

Going At It Alone

Soon after the MySpace incident, my grandfather passed away, and I was devastated. It was the first big death I had ever experienced, so I wasn't prepared for how it would feel. My grandfather had been sick with cancer for a very long time, and I visited him in the hospital regularly. One day, instead of me going to the hospital with my parents as usual, they dropped me at my other grandmother's house because I wanted to spend some time with her. On the ride home later, they broke it to me that my grandfather had died; even though I'd known that news was coming eventually, I felt completely blindsided by loss. Naturally, I blamed myself—that after all those visits, the *one* day I didn't go to see him ended up being the day that he died. And eventually, I saw the loss as a lesson that I should cherish every second I have with the people I love. But at the time, I

was crushed. I remember being in the church for his funeral, bawling and scream-crying. I couldn't help it.

By the time I went on winter break from school, my stress was compounded: I was upset about my grandpa, still shaken about what my online bullies had done, and dreading the idea of having to go back to a school where—at the time—I still didn't feel like I fit in. I told my parents I didn't want to go back, and luckily, they were supportive of my decision. So while my sister stayed in public school, I resumed homeschooling with my mom as my teacher.

With some of the pressure off, I was able to focus again, and completed schoolwork more efficiently. I liked getting work done, and I started to get addicted to that feeling of accomplishing things. It got to the point that I loved achieving my goals so much that if achieving my goals so much that if we stopped, *I'd* be the one asking my mother, "Mom, why are we taking a break? Why are we watching this movie? I want to work more!"

With all the extra time I had, I started to explore various creative avenues that I didn't have time to discover while enrolled in public school. I had to give up Pomerettes when I went back to homeschooling, so I filled the gap by performing in musicals through community programs and continuing to take dance classes. By participating in so many creative opportunities, I realized how much I enjoyed performing.

I remember my dance teacher was super-surprised when I performed at my first competition, because the second I got on stage, I was just *owning* it. We were dancing to Rihanna's "Pon de Replay" and you'd better believe we dressed up for it. I remember we wore these black low-rider pants and cobalt-blue crop tops with mesh arms. And we had serious "dance hair" too: it was slicked back into a ponytail with *at least* ten huge Swarovski crystals glued into the part—my mom had to use a special thin, tacky crayon tool to pick up the crystals and place them just right in the glue—and, of course, it was all topped off with about fifty pounds of hairspray to hold it all together. You know, just the usual outfit I wear when I go to Starbucks (kidding!). But that first time on stage was such a cool, special moment for me. Most of the people in the room had no idea who I was, and they were never going to see me again, so I felt free, like I could truly dance like no one was watching (cheesy, but true!). I went all in . . . and loved it.

Little did I know, though, I still had a big battle ahead of me as the year ahead would challenge my confidence and the happiness I was feeling would start to slip away.

When Anxiety Seeped In

The year after the MySpace incident, when I was twelve, I found out the main person who bullied me was a girl I knew very well, even though we hadn't gone to the same school. I thought we were friends! But for whatever reason—I don't know if she was jealous or just didn't like me—she seemed determined to hurt me in ways I hadn't known possible. And she did so bit by bit, through her actions over the course of a year.

One time, I was hanging out at a birthday party and the girl showed up with *my* best friend—and both of them ignored me. I wasn't surprised that my bully was ignoring me, but having my best friend ignore me? It felt like a

1 I think I was in sixth grade in this picture. 2 My purse was always filled with bubble gum and Tic Tacs at that age! I think we were at some casino in Reno, and I'm wearing my favorite shirt (which I wore practically every day—it was always dirty!). 3 My family threw me a surprise birthday party at the local pizza place—I thought I was showing up for a friend's party, so I wore my favorite black dress (naturally)! 4 All smiles on my tenth birthday. 5 Baby Beth! This was taken at one of my old houses. 6 So I know this is crazy, but this moment was definitely my first memory. I remember holding on to that bunny, which was one of my favorite Easter gifts. 7 I was definitely a tomboy growing up. Instead of playing dress up, I preferred to ride my bike inside the house (Mom was definitely mad!).

8 *Family time in Reno—we took a ton of casino trips growing up!* **9** *My sister and I are so close—here we are, goofing around in our backyard pool.* **10** *I'm not sure why I let that cat hang out with me. Although, I guess I'm napping, so did I even know the cat was there? Also, whose cat is that? I don't think it was ours . . .* **11** *I was twelve or thirteen here, and I had definitely just learned how to use the self-timer on my camera!* **12** *I'm not sure why I'm in that outfit when I was just hanging out at my grandma's!* **13** *Another shot of me as a baby, hanging out on Easter.* **14** *My mom often babysat this friend, who I admittedly was mean to from time to time!* **15** *Here I am at five years old, enjoying an ice pop at church after a wedding.* **16** *Celebrating my birthday with a good ol' game of Candyland!*

stab in my heart. I'll never forget the feeling of cold energy directed my way, especially from someone I thought was on my side. I was hurt and I was angry, but I didn't let it show.

Little things like that happened for months, as she took my friends and made up stories about me that would travel by word of mouth through people I knew and come back to me. It almost felt like *she* was the one controlling my life. I wasn't scared of her; I just felt powerless. I was always worried about what she was going to pull next. I became someone who was constantly stressed out, anxious, and insecure. And over time, those emotions just stuck with me in a variety of situations. Her actions may have triggered my fall but, for a while, I just kept on falling—and I couldn't get up.

My anxiety escalated quickly, and soon I couldn't function in social situations. One time, I was on the top floor of the shopping mall with my mom and when I approached the escalator to go down, I started to feel sick and said, "I have to sit down." And even though the rest of my family was inside the mall, I had to walk around the *outside* of the building to get back to them so I wouldn't have to go down the escalator. I know now that I was suffering a panic attack. After that day, I avoided stores and supermarkets for *five months* because I'd get so anxious being around a lot of people that I'd feel like I was about to pass out. There was just something about being

trapped in a crowd that made me feel like I wasn't in control. Eventually, just the fear of having another panic attack was enough to stop me from living my life.

And, with that, my bubble of places where I could go and things I could do began to get smaller and smaller. First, I couldn't hang out with family or friends. Then, I didn't even want to leave my house. And finally, even being inside my house, I began to have issues with eating. I got so anxious that I wasn't able to put food in my mouth for fear of what would happen if I tried to swallow. I would think, "What will happen if I swallow this? What if I *can't* swallow this?"

One day, all I ate was a pudding cup because I was so fearful of eating. And then I'd be upset with myself, confused as to why I was so afraid and just couldn't get over it. My own emotions were strangling my life; the most routine things would stress me out to the point of a panic attack.

That time was a really gray period for me. And the worst part of it all was that I truly thought that's how my life was going to go on. I was only thirteen years old by then—barely a teenager—but I felt like that was it for me, that I'd always, for the rest of my life, be too afraid to do anything. I've learned that's what happens with difficult times: We can get so caught up in the experience that it feels like that one moment is our new forever. Now, I know life doesn't work that way. But back then, I was starting to accept *my* life for what I thought it was: sad.

"Well," I thought, "there always has to be one person who is afraid to be in the world, right? I guess *I'm* that one."

Confined in the small world I created for myself, I began wasting a lot of time. Aside from school, all I did was watch TV, go on the computer, and sleep. Then I started watching videos. I first discovered YouTube two years earlier, when a friend told me to check out a now famously funny clip: Charlie Bit My Finger. Yep, that was the *very* first video I ever watched. After that I got into Fred and all of his hilarious stuff (the Fred Figglehorn character). Then, I watched a few beauty videos made by girls my age. And you know how when you watch one video on a certain topic, all the related ones come up? That's how I discovered that there was a ton of beauty and fashion content on YouTube. I wasn't even into beauty or fashion at the time, but the videos were so simple and

real, I found them calming and distracting in a good way. More than that, though, I was drawn to the idea that all these girls around the world were being creative and *making* something. With each new video I'd watch, I kept thinking about how amazing it was that each girl had posted this video for herself—no one posted it for her, and no one told her to do it. She posted it all on her own. And I loved that, together, these videos were all part of a larger whole—an entire *community*. And each girl was offering something important. So I just kept watching more and more. And then I started thinking about filming videos for myself. But the idea, at first, seemed as crazy as dancing in Beyoncé's next video. It seemed scary, but very freeing at the same time. Still, I didn't think I was *actually* going to do it . . . until one day, about a month later, when I found myself sitting across from a forward-facing camera, and pressing record.

Finding My Voice

As soon as I had the idea to make a video of my own, I shut it down. You know how sometimes you have crazy dreams that are so out there, you never intend to pursue them? It was like that.

Still, the idea of making videos stayed in

the back of my mind. So I took baby steps to see what it felt like by shooting videos on my BlackBerry. I would hold my phone out in front of me and film, talking so quietly that you couldn't even hear me in the playback. I

MY SECRET WEIRD FEARS

I know I can't be the only one who's scared of weird things. When I was little, for instance, I used to be afraid of balloons. For some reason, when other kids saw balloons at birthday parties, their first impulse was to pop them, and I'd get really stressed out about that! They'd even have balloon-popping contests, and I'd be like, "Uh, excuse me, why are we purposely trying to sit on balloons to make this awful surprise popping sound?!" That's why I hated birthday parties as a kid. Call me crazy, but I'm not kidding.

And when I was dealing with a lot of anxiety, I was really afraid of elevators; I was just like, "Nope, I'm not getting in that thing." I always assumed something was going to happen to the elevator, and we'd get stuck in there, and I wouldn't be able to breathe. That one was really rough because I would avoid elevators altogether, and in turn I would avoid places in general.

In fact, I remember when we went to visit my sister in college, realizing that you had to take an elevator up to her dorm, and surprise, surprise, I couldn't go up. I literally stayed by myself outside while my family went up to visit her. (Her room was pretty high up, and I wasn't about to climb up ten flights of stairs.) I was mortified having to wait at the bottom of the building for my parents. Eventually, I worked hard to overcome my anxiety, and my fear of elevators went with it. But there are two big things that do still scare me now.

didn't post any of them—and I deleted them afterward—but I just wanted to get the feel of it. I did that for a few months, until I got up the nerve to actually do it for real.

Even though most girls my age were wearing makeup, I was late to the party; I just wasn't into beauty products yet. So when I had the idea

for my first video, I asked my mom to take me to the mall so I could do my first makeup haul.

I didn't have a tripod or proper equipment yet, so I piled up a bunch of books and rested my family's Sony Handycam on top, before opening the curtains and blinds on my windows for lighting. Because I'd been practicing

FEAR #1: HITTING MY HEAD. I have this odd fear of hurting my head. It's my only big fear, and it's so weird: I'm afraid that I'll hit my head on the ground, or something will fall on it or knock it, and it will harm my brain—I guess it's because my mind is so valuable to me? But because I'm short (I'm five-foot-three), whenever I'm in a crowded area, I'm always protecting my head. (Okay, fine, not literally. You probably won't see me shielding my head with my hands at Sephora or shopping for helmets anytime soon. But I do look out for elbows, and I have my hands ready to go up if I need to block myself!) It used to hold me back from trying physical activities that involved going upside down. But now? I'll dive into almost anything, head first.

FEAR #2: BUGS. Certain bugs don't scare me and I'm cool with spiders, but flying bugs freak me out! I was on a hike with one of my guy friends, and he saw a spider and was panicking, and I was like, "Uh, do you want me to get it?" But if you put wings on that thing, I will run!

I'm learning, though, that when it comes to my fears, even if there's a slight, miniscule, minute possible risk of injury or death, I'd rather push through it and have the experience, instead of letting my fear hold me back. And so far, I've found that the more times I conquer my fears, the less I'm afraid of them. Trust me: Those knee-shaking, palm-sweating moments are worth it, because you never want a fear to stop you from living.

on my phone for so long, the first shoot went really well. The only funny thing is that I was trying so hard to make sure no one in my house could hear me, I was basically whispering. I did it in one long take, and I didn't film a second time.

I had no idea how to edit a video, so I plugged the camera into the computer and researched Windows Movie Maker. I chopped it all together, and to be honest, it was really bad quality. Still, I posted it.

It didn't get views right away, which I figured meant that no one was going to watch it. Then the view count started going up—first it was twenty-nine views, and then it was thirty. But that's when I realized something: A lot of those views were just mine because I kept refreshing it! But eventually, that video started to get other views. And about a week later, I made my second video. After my third, I reached about a hundred views.

At first my mom was the only one who knew I was doing YouTube, because I needed my parents' approval to start posting, and she eventually told my dad. My sister found out through the search history on the family computer (I didn't know about clearing it back then!), but she didn't say anything about it.

A few weeks later, I walked into a Fourth of July party to find all of my cousins watching my videos, and I was so nervous to find out their reaction! My dad's side of the family is really outgoing and loud, and here I was, quiet,

glasses-wearing Bethany, recording and posting videos online in which I looked completely different. It was like I was living a double life! But they said they thought it was cool.

I began to get very engaged with the YouTube community and would respond to anyone who commented on my videos. Then I started using Twitter to connect with people, and it all expanded from there. I didn't expect my viewership to skyrocket; I didn't even know that was possible.

Being successful at YouTube was never my intention. I just had fun making that first video, and knew I wanted to keep doing it— not for views, not for followers, but because I wanted to keep creating things. There was something so beautiful to me about having an idea and making it come to life, all on my own.

Now, Confidently Me

That first year of making videos, I felt so empowered. After going through some tough years where I felt like I didn't have control, I now had *all* of the control. And that's what I loved most about it. I could really express myself through editing, the music choices I made, and what I said; I could really make it *me*. And the more videos I created, the more

comfortable I felt being silly on camera and including bloopers.

I also started varying content: I created videos on hair, fashion, baking, and DIY. In a way, I was discovering myself through the videos I made. My channel has been the truest representation of me growing and changing. But it wasn't just me—my MotaFam was also growing up right along with me. In addition to

online. And what I learned through my laptop is also true in life: We all have full control over how we express ourselves and how we turn our experiences—good and bad—into something positive. YouTube helped me become the person I was meant to become. And once I made my mind up about who I wanted to be, I felt unstoppable—and I still do.

Ultimately, I'm grateful for my bullying experience. It was the hardest thing I've ever gone through, but it's what helped me break out of my shell. And that's been a big lesson I've carried in the years since: Sometimes the worst things you go through end up leading to the best things down the road. At one point, I was in a dark place and couldn't see the light at the end of the tunnel. But when I finally got to the other side, I was *better* for it. I doubted myself a lot growing up, and I spent a lot of time trying to change who I was, rather than living my life the way I wanted to live it.

A big hug to my MotaFam who continues to walk through this journey with me. I have finally found my own voice; my own style; my own health, beauty, and work routines—my own everything. And this is how I live.

Getting
MOTAVATED

*How I follow my passions,
find my confidence,
and feed my creativity*

Who we are is a direct response to the choices we make. If I'm not challenging myself and taking risks with my career and life goals, I feel like I'm missing out on the person I could be. There were times I doubted myself, but I followed my dreams anyway—and I'm glad I did. Things haven't always worked out—but I learn just as much from those moments in life, too. Whether you succeed or fail, shooting for the stars will show you what you're capable of.

I

Confidence

Each time we bravely express a new side of ourselves,
we reach a whole new level of confidence.

Blazing My Own Path

When I first started posting to YouTube, people would say, "Aw, that's cute, you make videos," in a tone that implied they weren't taking me seriously. Now people ask me how they can pursue a career online. In retrospect, I'm really glad I didn't let anyone else's ideas get into my head when I was first starting out. The coolest aspect of my work, in fact, is that the ideas are from *my* unique mind. It took me a while to grasp this concept, but it's a big one: No one has my way of thinking; no one will experiment with a DIY or recipe exactly the way I would; no one is going to have the same bizarre thoughts on a topic as me (and as you guys know, I have a *lot* of bizarre thoughts!).

Having my own channel allowed me to take what was swirling around in my brain and present it to the world the way only I could—or that you could, or that *anyone* could! The idea that each of us has something distinctive to offer inspired and propelled me.

My whole career on YouTube hasn't been about following other people, but about creating my own path. Navigating YouTube was challenging at times, because there was no guide or blueprint on how to become successful online. Most of the time, I was feeling my way through the dark, without anyone holding a flashlight ahead of me—and so, it's become a true test of trusting my vision. Now, if someone doesn't "get" what I'm working on or "get" what I want to do next, I don't worry about it.

Over the years, through all the projects I've worked on—from my videos to my clothing line to this very book—I can't always envision the end result, so I've gotten comfortable pursuing goals with unknown outcomes. But as confident as I've become, there are also situations where I feel so *uncertain* about what I'm doing, that it's freaked me out. It doesn't matter how much I've learned to embrace failure, I still have those moments where doubt slips in—and getting past those feelings takes practice.

RANDOM ME FACT: I CAN'T HELP BUT DIY WHAT I BUY

Rather than settle for a plain, normal desk accessory you pick up from an office store, I have a compulsion to DIY nearly every single thing I buy so it looks and feels more unique to me. I literally can't help it—I just want everything to look Pinterest-pretty! One time, for example, I wanted a desk caddy that would help me organize my work supplies, but instead of leaving it a dull gray, I sprayed it gold so it looked fresh and elegant on my white desk. And instead of settling for a mouse pad that wasn't totally my style, I made one by Mod Podge–ing some rainbow watercolor floral wrapping paper onto the underside of a clear plastic placemat. Of course, in my quest to make everything my own, the messy little Bethany in me still botches projects all the time. As long as I don't look at the backs and undersides of half of the things I make (that's where all the uneven, over-painted, badly glued parts are!), they still look beautiful to me.

My Work Style

When I want to feel confident at a business meeting or event, I like to wear really classic pieces that make me feel put together, but also very me. And my favorite work look always starts with a classic button-up because they're casual yet sophisticated, and very versatile. To make a button-up shirt look more professional, you can leave the sleeves down; if you want to look more relaxed, just roll them up. The buttons can shape your look, too: At a meeting, I'll always keep it buttoned higher; then, if I go out, I'll undo an extra button and add a necklace to give it a messy, chic vibe. Basically, if I'm wearing a button-up shirt, I feel like I have my life together. (If there was a Beth Thought Bubble above my head in a business meeting, it would say, "I may have been tired this morning, but I buttoned every single one of these buttons all by myself. Clearly, I'm on it!") Seriously though, I feel that with this one single item, you can make a solid first impression.

I tend to pair my dress shirts with dark wash jeans. Then, I'll switch up the look with a blazer or shoes, depending on the vibe I want. There are generally two styles I go for:

WORK STYLE #1: SOPHISTICATED

With my button-up and jeans, I'll add:

- A structured blazer. It adds a chic, down-to-business vibe. Sometimes, I like to bring in a pop of color with my blazer—my favorites are Topshop and Nordstrom. I even have a blazer cut like a cape: It has a serious-looking structure that works.

- Strappy sandals or heels. I like a mini-malist heel with just one strap around the ankle and one strap around the toe because they let your outfit do the talking—while elongating your leg. My go-to heels are by Stuart Weitzman in nude or black (seriously, I probably wear one of these pairs eighty percent of the time I wear heels).

WORK STYLE #2: EDGY

With my button-up and jeans, I'll add:

- A leather jacket. The button-up underneath keeps this look professional and put-together.

- A heeled boot with a little something extra—I have this one pair with a gold plate on the back of each heel that makes them unique.

Feeling Fear Is Normal

I used to wait until all of my fear disappeared before I tried anything that scared me—which of course, meant I never tried anything new at all. And how are any of us going to gain confidence if we stay holed up in our safe shells?

But then I realized, *the fear is always going to be there*. There's no such thing as being totally fearless. Fear comes with trying new things, and because it will never go away, we need to change how we see and experience it.

At the end of the day, fear is just emotion and energy. And, if anything, feeling fear is a sign that you might really *want* to do it. If a choice makes me feel something—even if it just brings on a case of the nerves—it usually means I care about it. If I'm working on something that doesn't make me as nervous, it usually means I'm not as invested in the outcome—and so, I won't get extraordinary results. So that's how I look at it now: If I'm scared, it means I care!

Out of the Way, Fear!

It was one thing for me to accept that a little fear monster would always be sitting on my shoulder while I worked toward my career goals; it was another to figure out how I could accomplish those goals in spite of it. And that epiphany came to me, well, with a splash. Let me explain.

When I was in Greece, my friends suggested we go for a morning swim, and while we were in the water, they suggested we walk up to the top of the cliff for a better view. As soon as we got to the top of the cliff, they dropped the real bombshell: My friends had jumped off of this very cliff yesterday, and as they leaped off a second time, they wanted me to take the plunge alongside them.

My heart started hammering a mile a minute, and my voice wavered as I told my friends I'd stand back and watch. The "Puh-lease, nice try" look they all gave me made me realize they weren't going to let me walk back down off that cliff—they were going to make me *jump* off.

I had never jumped off a cliff before, and I certainly hadn't been planning to that day. The fearful voice shouting in my head agreed. *"You're going to hit your head, Bethany. You should not be jumping off cliffs. You're supposed to live!"*

I know that this is natural; our minds are always in survival mode, protecting us from doing anything actually dangerous. Well, mine was protecting me up there for, like, forty-five minutes. We were up there so long, my friends started getting frustrated because we had things to do that day, and my nervous hesitation was holding us all up.

So, for a moment, I thought, "I'll just walk back down so we can get on with our day." But just before I backed off, I asked myself the one, big question I turn to in every moment I feel fear: "Do I *want* to do this?" And I had to be honest with myself: The answer was yes.

It's so simple, really. We get tied up with a tangle of terrified thoughts that distract us from the internal dialogue we should really be paying attention to: "Do I want to do it or not?" If the answer is yes, then, "Do I want to do it for myself, or am I being pressured into doing something I *don't* want to do?"

Now, if I had wanted to jump off the cliff just to impress my friends, I wouldn't have done it. But in this case, I knew deep down that it was going to help me personally, and that I was going to feel so great and amped up afterward. I knew I would regret it if I walked away.

So, an hour after climbing up onto that cliff, I jumped. And I was right; I felt alive and confident and ready to try something new. Because after all: If I can face my greatest fear, I can face anything.

I Love Neutral Nails

Because I go to so many work meetings and appearances, it's important that my nails always look polished. (And by "always" I mean that half the time my nails get chipped and I wait *way* too long to fix them and then they end up ruining some otherwise perfectly good selfies—but I do my best to keep them pretty!) I don't do designs on my nails very often, because in my opinion, busy nails can definitely distract from your outfit instead of complementing it. I find that this is especially true of professional outfits. Maybe my opinion of designed nail art will change (because being creative with your nails is really fun!), but these days, I keep my nails simple in three ways.

Square shape: Every once in a while, I play with other shapes (such as the pointier almond shape). But most often, I go with square, which feels clean and refined to me.

Neutral color: I tend to go for lighter colors, like creams and pinks. Sometimes I experiment with bolder colors, but neutral works best for work.

Short-ish length: I got nail extensions once, but they got in the way of everything—I had to bend my finger and use my knuckle to get my contact lenses out! So now, as much as I love long nails, I usually keep them fairly short, just past my fingertip.

Learning Not to Limit Myself

I was at a seminar about self-growth last year, and after a big day of listening to keynote speakers, we had the opportunity to go outside to the parking lot at night and face the heat, literally: I was offered the chance to test my courage by walking on hot coals—as in, hot coals that were, like, a thousand degrees—way hotter than the inside of an oven.

I waited in line to do it for a good forty minutes, all the while trying to mentally prepare myself to walk on the coals. When I got up there, though, I panicked. I looked the lady in the eye and said, "I can't do this. I just . . . I can't do it."

Then I started getting really emotional and crying a bit because I was so fired up to try it but I didn't feel like I had it in me. I was so disappointed in myself. So I started to walk off.

"Yes, you can," the woman said.

So I stopped. And I challenged myself. "Do I want to do it?" I knew the answer: I walked out there because I *wanted* to do it. And I wouldn't have walked outside to the parking lot and taken off my shoes if I didn't think I *could* do it.

"Think of that one thing that's been holding you back recently," the woman said, "that one thing that's been blocking you from moving forward." And there *was* something

that had been blocking me. The past two weeks, I'd been dealing with a lot of self-doubt about some projects I was working on. I was completely in my own head, overthinking my ideas and spiraling into a haze of confusion. One of the projects that was stressing me out was just a video I was working on, but for two weeks, I agonized over it. "The video's not good enough," I thought. "Why am I doing this? Why am I even a YouTuber? Who's going to watch this? Who do I think I am?" I was beating myself up, feeling horrible, and getting nowhere with any of it.

"Now," the woman said, "*let it go.*" And as soon as she said those three words—*let it go*—I was walking across those coals that were glowing orange in the night, looking up to the stars, and feeling an emotional high like I was on top of the world. I've never felt so energized in my entire life. I felt so alive, like I was a kid again!

Even though the whole walk was only a few seconds long I started to feel— unsurprisingly, I guess—the heat searing through my soles toward the end. The staff hosed my feet off on the other side, which helped. And while I did develop some blisters from it, I was so proud of myself for just doing it. The moment was huge for me because it reminded me about the power of our decisions. *I* made that decision. No one else did it for me. Our minds are machines and it's up to us to press the buttons. Now, whether I'm standing at the edge of hot coals or not, when I'm faced with a choice to stay stuck or move ahead, I think of that moment and go, "Oh, it's just a decision to let my anxious feelings go."

I have a friend who didn't walk on the coals that day. And afterward, I wondered if she regretted not doing it, so I finally asked her.

"No," she said, "I had no desire to do it. I didn't even take my shoes off when I left the building."

"Why?" I asked her.

"I didn't think it would help me," she said. "I knew I wouldn't need that experience to grow."

That exchange confirmed, at least for me, that the question we should ask ourselves before taking a risk is twofold: It's not just about whether you *want* it, it's also about asking yourself if the experience will help you grow.

The Beauty of Glasses

I first got glasses when I was about seven or eight, and though I was happy I could actually see clearly, I was not into being "the girl with the glasses" all the time. It was one thing to wear them all day in school, but later when I started taking dance classes, it was a whole different story. I loved being on stage, wearing an amazing, sparkly costume—but then I would have to put my glasses on with it. And even though most people weren't paying the slightest bit of attention to what I felt were two monstrous lenses on my face, I still felt different. And hey, to be honest, I really just wanted everyone to look at my tutu and sequins instead.

School was all about fitting in and looking like everyone else, yet I felt *so* different. The school administrators tried to help kids like me by creating the Glasses Club. If I didn't want to go outside to play at recess, I could join other glasses-wearing students in a classroom to read books or play games, which I did a few times. (By the way, I had completely forgotten about the Glasses Club until *just* now while writing this down; I can't believe I forgot about something as bizarre as that!) No one ever teased me about wearing them— and, to be honest, I preferred reading to recess anyway—but it was only a slight help in what felt like

a big gap between the other kids in my class and me.

My glasses really got in the way when I began making my early YouTube videos, because I didn't want to film in them. This meant I had to take my glasses off as soon as I started filming, set them by my side, and as soon as I said, "Bye," grab them and put them back on. The uncut videos back then always included the funny five seconds at the start and finish when I was dealing with my glasses. Not only that, but I also had to look in the viewfinder to see if the product was reading on camera, so you can *totally* tell in those early videos that I was squinting when I

held something up, because I couldn't see the viewfinder to save my life!

While I do wear my contacts a lot, I'm not embarrassed about my glasses anymore because they make me who I am. I couldn't help the eyesight I was born with, so I had a choice: I could either hide the fact that I'm a glasses girl, or I could embrace it and make the most of it, which was not only easier, but more fun. Now, if anything, I *purposely* wear them to make an outfit look even better.

Here are the four makeup elements I combine with my glasses to make one confidently gorgeous look:

1. *Bold your brows.* I'll outline and fill in my brows with a brow pencil so they balance the boldness of the frames.

2. *Define your eyes.* I will smudge a chocolate-brown pencil under my lash line to make my lashes stand out, or I'll do a thickly winged liner to help my eyes pop through the lenses.

3. *Warm your cheeks.* I'll go for a warm, peachy bronze hue, blushed high on my cheekbone. It's just enough to add some defining color without competing with my eyes.

4. *Mute your lips.* I will wear a muted lip color—like a soft pink, or a grayish lavender—again, to keep the focus up on the glasses and avoid competition (having too much going on is never a good look!).

Desk Inspo: What I Love About My Desk Space

There are a few elements I need in my workspace to get inspired and conquer my goals.

Natural light: My workspace has to be really bright, with white walls and a lot of natural light, so it feels very crisp and clean.

A cozy feel: Feeling cozy is important to me because it makes me want to stay put—and if I don't leave the room, I get more done! For instance, if I get tired working in a chair, I will lounge on my super-marshmallow-y white couch, which keeps me in the work zone.

Pops of bright color: While the base of my office is white, I like to add accents I can easily rotate in and out. (If I added a permanent color, like wall paint, let's be real, I would be so sick of it in a month. And who has time to repaint their walls every four weeks?!) Currently, I have pops of greens, pinks, and florals, and one of my pillows has palm trees on it, giving the space a slight tropical vibe.

A white desk is my blank canvas: I love my clean, white desk. It has a glass top, so I'll put colorful notebooks and photographs underneath it for fun.

Inspirational collages: I like to have something motivational around me when I'm working. Tacking up an inspirational collage is an easy way to create a beautiful, warm, inviting atmosphere for my viewers. One time, for instance, I hung printed photos from Instagram and Tumblr on my wall in the shape of a heart.

Fairy lights: I've strung fairy lights in my workspace for a relaxing, pretty atmosphere. The more soothing my workspace, the less I stress—and the less I stress, the more work gets done!

Calming candles: Candles are a big thing for me, and I tend to use them like a scent scrapbook: I'll burn the same one signature candle scent for a year or two, so that when I smell it again years later, it will take me right back to that place. (You know what I'm talking about, right? It's so cool how that happens!) My current fave: the Volcano candle from Anthropologie.

Behind the Scenes:
When I Recorded My First Song

I've had dreams of singing my whole life. But singing is scarier to me than making videos, because when I'm reviewing a product on camera, it's easy for me to be open and honest. At the end of the day, someone else made the lotion, or foundation, or body spray. When I'm filming, focusing the attention on a product I didn't have a hand in creating alleviates some of the pressure I put on myself, to be honest. But singing? That's a whole different ball game, because I'm putting *myself* out there for the world to critique.

Even though I loved to sing, any time someone would bring up the idea of recording music, I dismissed it immediately. I wasn't sure about how good my voice was, so I didn't even want to go there. Plus, I often told myself that Bethany is into fashion and beauty and lifestyle, not music. (And when Bethany refers to herself in the third person, Bethany listens!) I pushed it to the side and kept going about my normal routine.

Then my friend Mike Tompkins, a singer and music producer, reached out to me about recording a song together called "Need You Right Now." I was ready to dismiss the idea like I always did. But the more I thought about

it, the more I realized that the only reason I thought I couldn't do it was because I had never *tried*. So I decided I wanted to go for it.

Recording the song was so intimidating. I'd never been in a recording studio before, so I didn't know what to expect. I went in at night, which I'm assuming was the only time slot the studio had available. Being in the recording room by myself felt really weird; while I could see the studio producers through a big glass window, I couldn't always hear them. Being alone in that tiny box, I felt raw, vulnerable, and under enormous pressure—it was like, "Okay, you want to sing? You're up. Let's see what you can do."

I put on the headphones and started singing. At first I was like, "Whoa, that's my voice!" And for the first thirty minutes, I was definitely shaky. It took about two or three hours to record the song. They'd have me do certain parts over, and then they'd cut off the sound in my headphones so I couldn't hear them while they talked to each other on the other side of the glass, so of course I was like, "Hello?! What are you talking about?!"

When we finished recording, I sat on the couch in the studio and they replayed the whole song for me. It was like an out-of-body experience. Sure, I'd recorded and played back my own voice on my iPhone before, but hearing it that day in the studio? It was incredible. They turned the song up louder than I'd ever heard music played before, and it sounded out of this world. In that one moment, my dream became a reality for me—and in a truly new way. After years of being completely in control of my creative process in a field I knew so well with YouTube, this was the first time I had to rely on *other* people to make my goal happen. I felt so vulnerable because there was so much I didn't know. Stepping into a world I was completely unfamiliar with meant I had to relinquish some of my creative power and defer to these people's skills and experience to guide me. I was proud of myself for that accomplishment—and excited to be able to watch, listen, and learn.

A couple of weeks later, after they went through the process of finalizing the song, I got scared. "I don't want to release it!" I told my dad. "What if my viewers hate it?" I almost tried to call it off, but it was too late for that.

It went up on iTunes, and we also put up a lyric video on my channel. And then I waited.

Finally, the viewers started responding—- and they loved it. That moment was one of the most rewarding of my entire career, hands down. I was on top of the world! It reminded me how capable I am of succeeding at anything I set my mind to—-how capable we *all* are. It also reminded me that we have so many different sides of ourselves and it's important to honor all of them. Sure, I could have listened to the voice that told me to stick to what I knew I was good at and just keep making videos. But I couldn't ignore the fact that I have so many other passions I want to pursue, too—and just like I jumped into that icy blue water in Greece, I knew I just *had* to take the leap and follow my dream to sing. Recording that song showed me I should be pursuing all of my passions, even in areas people might not expect from me. And once I started to get out of my own way and just do it, I learned that when we bravely express a new side of ourselves, we reach a whole new level of confidence.

My Favorite Green Smoothie

On a day packed with meetings, my smoothies get my energy going and keep me motivated throughout the day. This recipe is like a power booster to get things done!

INGREDIENTS
ice cubes
½ banana
1 cup kale
½ cup cut pineapple
⅓ cucumber
optional: spinach, or another green veggie
¼ cup water

TO MAKE THE SMOOTHIE
Step 1: Combine the ice, banana, kale, pineapple, and cucumber, and, if you want, whatever extra green you're feeling, like spinach. I like to mix it up. Add the water and blend until smooth.

Step 2: Drink to feel refreshed and energized!

My Most Nervous Moment Ever

I think it's safe to say that I have never been more nervous in my entire life than when I interviewed President Barack Obama at the White House.

For the interview, three of us YouTuber creators (Hank Green, GloZell Green, and me—I felt pretty lucky they let me come even though I wasn't a "Green"!) were invited to interview the President for our channels, to address the issues our viewers cared about. We would mimic our YouTube setups in small stations with temporary walls, rugs, and chairs that were arranged inside a big room at the White House; the President was going to stop at each one for about twenty minutes each.

I spent weeks researching topics to discuss and asking my online audience what they wanted to know. I did my final revisions on the questions once I got to Washington, DC, writing them all down on note cards. The White House helped us prepare further by doing a trial run in a warehouse the day before. They even constructed our sets with us and brought in—get this—a fake president! Fake President Obama sat down with each of us while we ran through the questions on our note cards; because it was going to be a live interview the next day, this was our chance to work through any issues. The thing was, when Fake President Obama sat down for the run-through, I was shaking so hard I could hardly hold my cards. My mind was racing: If my confidence was this rattled with a fake President, what in the world would I be like with the *real* one?!

The next day, when the time came for the real interview inside the White House, I was terrified—I was also third, so by the time he sat down, my fear had built up insanely in my head. I was so nervous that I had to hold my hands so they would stop shaking. Even my *lips* were shaking. But what's funny is, once we got talking, I got it together and the conversation flowed very naturally. I asked him how he planned to make college more affordable and how we could better prevent bullying. Then I admitted how I'd never really followed politics much before this interview—like many people of my generation—so I asked him, "Why should the younger generation be interested in politics?" I thought he had the best answer: He explained that we need to be involved in making decisions for the future because *we* will be the ones living in it! It made so much sense and really opened my eyes to how important it is to vote and have a say in the decisions our country makes. Through it all, the President was so easy to talk to that it felt like we were just hanging out, having a good time—which

is why I just *had* to ask him at the end if he'd take a selfie with all three of us. (And if I do say so myself, it was a darn good one!)

Afterward, I was *sure* I had messed it up, and I was ready for people to pick up on every nervous tremble. Instead, they left comments like "Wow, Bethany, you were so poised and so calm." I was so surprised! Apparently, when I'm very nervous about something on the inside, people don't notice it on the outside. (I think I'm just *so* nervous and scared that I go the opposite direction: I zen myself out, and appear very calm and relaxed.)

I still look back on it now, thinking, "Did that really happen? Did I *really* get a selfie with the President?" The whole experience really showed me how our inner feelings don't always surface on the outside. So just because I feel terrified to step into a new situation, I can still barrel through those feelings with confidence. Knowing that, I now feel stronger and more assured each time I step up to try a new, nerve-wracking experience. But trust me: If I'm doing something scary like interviewing the President of the United States? You'd better believe I'm gonna be shaking in my heels!

What I Do When I Don't Feel Confident

As confident as I've become in my career, I face small hurdles all the time. For example, I know my viewers wish I'd put up videos more often, so I get stressed about making them wait for one. When I started trying to understand the pressure I was putting on myself to make amazing videos more quickly, I realized this: My "stress" is really just an underlying fear of disappointing my viewers.

I've never really admitted that fear of disappointing them out loud (or whatever the written equivalent of "out loud" is). I already knew that I sometimes set standards for myself that are unrealistic. But when I dive further into my feelings (whoa, I'm getting deep here, guys!), the truth is that I feel like if I work really hard on something and it doesn't work out, I'm letting people down. So instead of getting my hopes up and letting others—and myself—down, I'll procrastinate. I'll say, "I have other things to do, anyway," or "It's not the right time for me to do this right now." But deep down, it's not that I don't have the time.

What I've learned is that it's much easier to say, "I'm stressed," than it is to say, "I'm afraid." It's really just my ego talking. I think

as a society, a lot of us turn to the excuse of being overwhelmed because "stress" feels like a strong, brave, important word, while "afraid" feels like a weak one. But the faster you peg what's really going on, the easier it is to move forward—even when that means letting some of your perfectionism go.

For instance, I make a lot of videos I know my viewers will want—like personal Q&A videos and room tours—that get a great response online. But every now and then, I want to post something different to mix it up, like a travel video where I've gotten to film some beautiful outdoor landscapes. The result is still positive, but I know even before I post it that it's not going to get the same response that the other videos do. And that's okay! Because posting videos about various topics—not just one or two—makes *me* happy. So I post those with confidence.

I look at the end result of things differently now. I don't think of anything as "a failure." Instead, I'll just consider it "not turning out how I expected it to." True accomplishment isn't about a perfect result or the most "likes." It's the fact that you did it at all.

How I ... Choose a Dress for Work

When I wear a dress to something work-related, I always choose a structured style that holds more shape, so it doesn't look too casual. One of my favorite looks is a structured long-sleeve dress that hits above the knee, paired with knee-high boots. My other favorite look is pairing a structured short-sleeve dress with chunky stacked heel sandals and a leather jacket. Both looks are dressy but not too formal, so I still feel like me.

SNACKS ON-THE-GO

If I know I'm going to be in meetings all day, I'll pack a little snack to keep my energy up. Here are my favorites:

FRUIT. Bananas are my go-to. But I might also bring apples, peaches, tangerines, or little clementines.

NUTS. I'll bring raw or unsalted roasted almonds (they're crunchier!) in a bag because they're so filling and good for you.

GRANOLA BAR. I don't eat these often because they're high in sugar, but if I'm starving between meals, a granola bar can save me from eating everything in sight later on. Lightly snacking throughout the day keeps your body satisfied—and prevents you overeating at your next sit-down meal!

My Best 3 Busy-Day Hairstyles

I take special care to do my hair for a busy day of work—or as Beyoncé would say, for *werk*. (Oh my gosh, did I seriously just make that bad pun? But it's true!) Hair complements my look as much as what I'm wearing does. And I always feel more put together and confident when I take the time to create a professional-looking style.

All of my work styles start with dry hair. When my hair is wet, I'll spray in some Matrix Turbo Dryer Blow Dry Spray, then blow it dry using a hair dryer and a flat wet brush to style it. When my hair is almost dry, I'll bend over, flip my hair upside down and blow-dry the roots for more volume. Once I've done all that, I'll continue styling in one of these three ways.

#1: CURLED AND CUTE

Step 1: I start with a texturizing blow dry spray or a dry shampoo like the one from Drybar—not to get rid of oil, but to give my strands a more textured feel. The more texture your hair has to begin with, the better it will hold a curl.

Step 2: I part my hair on the left side and curl every piece, using the T3 Twirl Wand from Sephora. (I used to use the T3 Whirl Trio Wand, but I accidentally sat it next to plastic, and the result was a big, plasticky, melted-on mess! So now I have a new one with a clamp. It takes me about five minutes longer to use the clamping wand, but I find it gives me a more structured curl.)

Step 3: I stop curling each section as soon as I get toward the tip of my hair, leaving the very ends alone, which keeps the curls looking natural.

#2: STRAIGHT AND SERIOUS

Step 1: I spray the blow dry spray into my hair to give it texture and protect it from the heat of my straightening tool.

Step 2: I then tease my roots with a comb before I start my straightening, which gives my hair a little more volume. (Though if I want pin-straight hair from root to tip for a strong, getting-things-done vibe, I'll skip this step.)

Step 3: I'll use my straightening wand, the T3 Single Pass hair-straightening tool, to go over small sections of hair, bit by bit. There's no science to which sections I do first or last; I just make sure to run my wand slowly over each one so there are no rogue waves.

#3: FULL AND FUN

Step 1: After a spritz of blow dry spray, I pull a small section of hair and clamp it in my straightening iron. For the first inch, I straighten normally.

Step 2: Here's the cool part: About two inches down from my root, I'll rotate the straightening iron 180° away from my head, as if I'm folding my hair in half (if it's in my right hand, for example, I'll rotate the straightener counterclockwise). Then, with the straightener *still sideways*, I run the tool all the way down my hair.

Step 3: Repeat until all of your hair has gone through the straightening iron. Even though I've only added that one single rotation to each strand, it gives my hair overall textured, messy waves.

Getting Confident for a Meeting

I used to get really nervous before interviews and meetings—the same way I'd get nervous when I was in school and about to do a presentation in front of the class. Whether you're in school, doing an interview for college, or talking to someone about a work internship, here are my top four ways to boost confidence:

First, I'll ask myself, "What are my opinions on the topic we'll be discussing?" I never try to come up with something to say specifically beforehand; I sound really robotic when I speak from a script. Instead, I'll just think, "Where do I stand on this issue? How do I feel about it?" And that's it. Then, instead of nervously preparing what to say next in my head, I'm able to be present and participate in the discussions at hand.

Then, I focus on what I have to offer. I like to remind myself what I can bring to the particular job or project. So I'll think, "What makes me unique here?" Sometimes, you'll realize that you have a skill no one else in the room has—and that can be a very valuable card to hold.

In interviews and meetings, it's not just about what you say, but how you're saying it. In the past, I would hunch over and speak meekly, like I was asking a question. But how can you believe in someone who doesn't believe in herself? So I stand strong. I'll hold a tall posture, look a potential business partner (or classmate, or teacher, or interviewer) in the eye, and speak with a confident tone. If you haven't mastered this yet, practice makes perfect: The bathroom mirror is your friend!

Finally, I keep an open mind. I used to go into meetings hoping I'd be offered something that might advance my career—the same way a job or acceptance letter from a top university would. And if the meeting didn't lead to something big afterward, I'd feel down about it. Now I go into it with an open mind—because whether the sit-down leads to something positive or not, you might learn something. A meeting that might feel useless could teach you something for your next interview—or, might show you what *not* to do. Ultimately, instead of relying on other people to offer me my next step, I stay focused on what *I'm* doing to get to where I want to be.

A FUNNY STORY:
"MY FIRST AWKWARD MEETING"

I've had some awkward meetings over the years. Often it's because I've forgotten someone's name and I can't concentrate on anything else. (Or, I'll call someone by the completely wrong name. Oops.)

But my most embarrassing meeting was when I had a really weird handshake at the end. We had a good meeting, so as we got up to leave, I was thinking, "I don't know if you want a handshake or a hug, but since we had a really good meeting, I'm going in for a hug!" I couldn't help it. But as I leaned forward, he stuck his arm out between us to go for a bro handshake. I remember both of us being really quiet because we both felt weird about it. But what I really wanted to do was crack up. Instead, I kept on my serious face, then laughed about it later while telling my friends. And that's why—believe it or not—I'm *glad* when awkward moments happen, in work interactions and beyond. Take another example, which happened outside the office, when my friend and I barged into the wrong hot yoga class.

We had gotten there so early that the previous class of about twenty people was still finishing up their last ten minutes of stretching. Thinking it was our class, we marched right to the front of the room.

"Wrong class," the teacher said to us. But we didn't hear him, so we started setting up our yoga mats between all the students, all fresh and ready to stretch. At that point, the teacher had to look right at me and shout, "Wrong class, honey!"

So we rolled our mats back up and raced out of there. But instead of being embarrassed, we were hysterically laughing. Because whether it's work or play, in public or in private, mortifying moments are good for us. So if you ever feel like a turtle wanting to crawl back into your shell after an awkward interview or experience in class, I suggest taking the opposite approach: Be grateful you have a hilarious new tale that will make your friends laugh. Really, what's life without a good, embarrassing story to tell?

Refresh and Rejuvenate: My 10 Best "Wake Up, Beth!" Beauty Secrets

For all those mornings I feel exhausted but still have to (somehow . . .) get myself up, my face fresh, and my mind ready for the day, I'll turn to one of these beauty tricks to help transform how I look and feel.

MY 2 BIG TRICKS . . .

The Freezing Spoon Trick: If I wake up with puffiness under my eyes, I use frozen spoons to fix it.

How it works: Keep spoons in the freezer. In the morning, close your eyes and rest the round side of the cold spoons on your lids for ten to twenty minutes. Not only does it de-puff, it boosts circulation to the delicate skin around your eyes, making you look bright-eyed and ready for the day. Bonus points: The freezing cold really jump-starts your morning!

The Splash Mask Trick: The Blithe Korean splash mask from Glow Recipe is one of the best things I've ever discovered and is an absolute morning-saver. I have all three scents, but lately I've been using the Energy Yellow Citrus & Honey one the most.

How it works: Pour a cap full of liquid formula into a sink full of water, then repeatedly splash it on your face for thirty to sixty seconds. I'll use it in the shower, too: After I wash my hair, I pat a capful on my face for thirty seconds. It makes your skin so soft, tight, clean and awake, like you just left the spa.

. . . AND 7 LITTLE TIPS

White eyeliner: Line your waterline with white eyeliner to brighten your eyes. For even more radiance, add a touch of white eyeliner (or light, shimmery shadow) to your inner corners.

Concealer: I use NARS liquid concealer, two shades lighter than my foundation, to cover up proof of my exhaustion: dreaded dark circles!

Lash curling: Curling my lashes opens up the eyes a lot.

Blush: It helps to add color if your face is dull from lack of sleep.

Beauty balm: I'll dab a face balm, like the Magic Balm from Honest Beauty, above my lip and on the apples of my cheeks. Whenever I do this, people always ask me what I've done to make my skin glow!

Dry shampoo: It gives tired, flat sleep-hair more volume.

Curl your hair: I'll go through my hair with a curling wand to give it messy but pretty bedhead waves.

My Confidence Accessory: Sunglasses

My reflective sunglasses are a powerful statement piece. Before a meeting, I'll take them off and put them on my shirt so that, in a way, they end up looking like a cool necklace. I'm currently obsessed with mirrored, aviator-style glasses, like the Dior Reflected pair I recently invested in. They go with every outfit, and I know they will last. Granted, when I say *every* outfit, there may be some exceptions. Sometimes sunnies don't have a place in a nine-to-five office environment, so you really just have to read the room. But for me, I feel like they give me a strong, mysterious edge.

Boldly Reaching for My Goals

I've never really been into New Year's Resolutions, because if there's something I want to do, I start doing it. *Now.* The way I see it, if I'm not ready to switch something up, there's no point forcing it —because it will never become an enjoyable habit. Still, I have so many goals; I have to figure out which one to go for next. So here's how I choose.

First, if a goal starts to materialize in my mind, I'll write it down in one of my notebooks—and I'm very direct with how I write a goal down. For example, when I wanted to create a clothing line, I wrote, "Create a clothing line" or just "clothing line." I always express my goals in a way that's super-clear, and as big as I can get.

Then, if I think about that same goal again, I'll rewrite it in the same notebook; I'll just flip to a different page and write it neater, or in a different color. I find that through the repetition, certain goals rise to the top. It's like by seeing them again and again, they become solidified and, on some level, attainable.

Aside from my big goals, I will write down smaller goals, too. Like "Take the TV out of your room" or "Stop watching TV before bed" (both of which I've done). Because if I tell myself I'm gonna do it, *I'm gonna do it.*

THE JUMPING JACK TRICK FOR GOALS

I discovered something cool during one of my aerial classes. Aerial, if you don't know, is that circus-looking performance where you hold on to fabrics hanging from the ceiling, then do all sorts of twirls and moves on them. The very first time I tried it was terrifying; I'd never done anything like it, so newbie me had to call on my courage to get me through my first lesson. Now, more than a year later, I'm nowhere near an expert at it (trust me!), but I took it on as a challenge and have fun pushing myself.

Anyway, one day, I was in aerial class, and I couldn't do a move. I tried and tried and was going to keep forcing it until I got it. But my coach had a different idea.

"Get down from there," she said, "walk into the kitchen, and do ten jumping jacks." She literally had me step out of the room to do it. And the whole time I was doing my jumping jacks, I was thinking, "Why are you making me do this? This is weird." But when I went back in and tried the move again, I did it. Easily.

I've learned the same thing works in my creative process: Sometimes if I'm stuck, I'll step away and go to the beach, or take a little road trip to give myself some distance from the goal. Or, I guess I could do some jumping jacks! Whatever it is that you do, refocusing on something different really shifts your perspective and gets you out of your own head, so you're able to step back to whatever it is you were doing and nail it.

The Scariest Thing I Do

One of the most terrifying things I do—scarier than walking into a room full of executives, even—is speak in front of high school and middle school students. The reason it's unnerving is because students are forced to be there, so I know when I go up on that stage, they're probably thinking, "Why am I here? This is boring." And I get it; I was a teenager just a few years ago, feeling just as bored with anything I was forced to sit through.

So I do the only thing I can do: be me. But it hasn't been easy figuring that out! A couple of years ago, I was on stage in Australia with a girl who had a big personality. I was anxious I wouldn't be able to live up to the energy she was giving off, and my insecurity was getting the best of me. But instead of faking more energy or falling back into the shadows, I just thought, "I don't want to steal what *she's* doing, so what's the best *I* can do?" And it all worked out, as our energies helped balance each other.

Growing up, I never thought I could speak in front of people. I never had a chance to experiment with it—let alone get to a place where I felt like I owned it. It took time for me to get more comfortable with it, but now I enjoy speaking in public. Here are my favorite ways to get myself prepared to give a presentation or speak in front of an audience:

I get amped up first. I try to get myself in a good mood with music, while thinking about what I'm grateful for.

I talk about my personal story. I've noticed that once I start sharing what's personal to me, students become more engaged, their body language loosens up, and they start sharing their own stories. Here's the thing: Everyone in an audience is going through something difficult, to some degree. The more personally you can connect, the better.

I try to look at as many people as possible. A lot of people say to focus on one person, but I don't like to do that; I like to connect with everybody. So I look everyone in the eye for a couple of seconds if I can.

I express my strong convictions. Your audience will feel your positive energy if you believe in what you're saying and you're passionate about your message. When I focus on my conviction in what I'm saying, as opposed to the audience's reaction, my nerves just fall away and my confidence shines.

2

Creativity

You can face what's freezing you, push past it, and create something great.

Following My Passion

I first got into YouTube because I loved being creative and I was passionate about making videos. I saw it as a fun hobby. So as weird as it sounds, when it started to grow and I was approached by brands, I almost didn't want my videos to grow into a career!

I worried that if it became a job or business, I would lose my passion for it. I guess I always thought work was supposed to *feel* like work, so if I was having fun with it, it couldn't be my job. Now I know better. It is definitely possible to be passionate about something and make it your business—I'm living proof.

Finding your passion can be hard. But if you're able to figure out what drives you and creatively turn that into a career—for me it was YouTube, for others it could be writing, or making pottery, or playing professional soccer, or building computer programs—you're going to love your work. And that usually lends itself to greater success.

How to Become a Successful YouTuber

Once my videos started getting popular, the first thing people would ask me was how to become a successful YouTuber. But I don't think that's the right question. And I'll tell you why.

My first intention was never to become a successful YouTuber, and I don't think I would have made it to where I am now if it had been. When I started, I was just so excited to be making videos, I spent every minute of the day researching new ways to film and edit. Because I loved the process so much, I was always asking myself, "How can I improve my next video?" My love for creating content has always been the driving factor behind my channel, and I wouldn't be where I am today if it wasn't for that drive.

So I think if your intention is "I want to get this many views" or "I want this many subscribers," you might not reach the goal because your heart isn't in the experience itself. Your love for what you do will propel you toward success—no ifs, ands, or buts about it. And take it from me: Even if you don't love what you're doing in the *moment*—like studying for a test that's required for you to graduate and get going on your larger goals, or practicing a computer skill that will eventually make your work easier—your drive for the goal you've set for yourself can be the real reward.

The Weirdest Thing I Did to Get the Shot

I'm sure a lot of creative people will understand that when I want to film something specific, I'll do whatever it takes to get the shot. But one time, I took filming to a really embarrassing level—I've honestly been trying to forget it!

I was doing a video on fall fashion, and I had this idea for the intro that I would show the transition from summer into fall by filming myself going to bed in the summer, and waking up in a fall wonderland full of leaves. The timing was tight: I had to film and upload it within two days, but I was headed to Toronto for work. So I packed a blowup mattress, a pajama dress, and a package of fake leaves in my suitcase (yes, I am crazy, and I love it) to film on location.

When I got to my hotel in Toronto, I changed into my pajamas, inflated the mattress, borrowed some sheets and a pillow from my hotel, and headed out with a friend to find a place to film. We found a small park where we set up and made the bed on the ground, then sprinkled a ton of fake leaves everywhere. But just as I climbed into the bed, the cops arrived and told us we couldn't film there. We tried to talk them out of it, but we couldn't get the footage!

So I picked up the mattress and bedding, collected the fake leaves, and walked it all back to the hotel. Desperate to get the shot, I asked the front desk if we could borrow a patch of grass to film on. They agreed, so we set up the whole shoot all over again, except this spot was even busier than the park! Through the camera lens, it looked like we were in a private area having this dreamy experience, but the truth is that people were walking up and down the path next to it the entire time. And because my friend was filming it all with a tiny camera that was hard for others to see, people were staring at us, like, "What is this girl doing? Why is she in a bed in her pajamas . . . with fake leaves . . . *outside*?" I think they thought I was literally sleeping on the hotel grounds. It's so embarrassing, but I guess it goes to show how determined I was for the creative cause!

Behind the Scenes: I Mess Up a Lot (Like . . . a Lot!)

When you have four hours of footage and need to edit it down to just a few minutes, you can imagine there is a lot that goes on in those extra takes. And since I've uploaded hundreds of videos over the years, trust me, there have been a lot of mess-ups. Though there are plenty I don't remember (I think my brain is trying to protect me from my former humiliations!), there are some mistakes in particular that burn bright in my memory, from beauty flubs to filming issues to DIYs that didn't work out.

In the very beginning, when I was fourteen, I was only giving makeup tips, even though I'd never done my makeup before. (I had to learn from *other* YouTubers how to do it!) When I was filming myself, I couldn't do my makeup in front of my big mirror, because it would block the lens, so I either had to work with a small compact on the table, or do it blindly. I remember one time, I was crouched over doing my eyeliner, and when I came up to show the camera, I saw in the viewfinder that I had a piece of eyeliner pencil stuck on my eyeball! I was so freaked out, I was like, "I'm blind, that's it!"

Once, I did a video showing how to do a tie dye–like marble nail art technique, and it was not as easy as I'd thought it would be. It involved dripping different nail polish colors in water, mixing the drips with a toothpick, then laying your finger in it to create a cool swirly pattern on your nails. But when I first tried it, the paint got all over my fingers, and it looked like an eight-year-old had painted my nails! So I had to do it all over, and in the final video, I added a step where you tape your skin around the nails first with Scotch tape.

Another time I tried to film a nail video, I thought it would be fun to film outside in my family's backyard, but in the middle of doing it, a bee flew into my nail polish and I freaked out (flying bugs, remember? They're so scary!). I was like, "Nope, I'm out. Filming this again tomorrow indoors."

I'd like to say I have a folder full of my funny bad clips, or videos I never finished and uploaded, but I was really bad at backing things up back in the day and I deleted them all. Now I like to save my videos on an external hard drive, and more often than not, I also include my goofs and mess-ups. Because the minute I started to share those bloopers in my videos, everything changed.

MY FAVORITE VIDEO COLLAB EVER

My favorite collaboration was when Tyler Oakley and I dressed up as Miranda Sings. I love doing the Miranda Sings voice and pretending to be her, so when Tyler suggested we do a parody of her (after all, imitation is the sincerest form of flattery), I was all in. We called Miranda for some advice on how to be her. Predictably her best tip of advice was "You will never be me! Don't try!" I think we got pretty close, though: We changed into the signature Miranda button-up and high-waisted red sweatpants, added "lisstick" (duh), clipped our hair back (Tyler wore a wig!), and did some Miranda twerking. I know I'm biased, but I think we sounded just like her . . . it was hilarious!

HOW I . . .
MAKE A YOUTUBE VIDEO

The quality of my videos has changed a lot through the years, so these days it takes a lot longer to film and edit a video than it did at the beginning. But here's how I usually get a video done, from the first spark of an idea to the upload.

STEP 1: IDEAS

HOW I GET IDEAS. My ideas come from a combination of places, and I'll collect them on Pinterest or in folders on my computer. Online, I'll look at blogs, other people's Pinterest boards, and search Google images for what I'm working on to see what's already been done. I'll flip through current magazines. I'll go to the mall and see what's on the clothing racks. I've even gotten inspired in grocery stores, seeing what foods I could use for beauty or DIY ideas. If there's something I'm really loving—like, if I discover a new makeup technique or a new way to do my hair—I figure other people might enjoy it, too.

STEP 2: FILMING

HOW I FILM. The shooting process can be unpredictable, but it generally takes two to three days to film one video. I like to block out "filming days"; for example, I won't schedule anything on Monday/Tuesday so I can *film film film*—say, shooting half the video on one day, and the second half the next. I only plan my shoots a couple of weeks in advance of the planned upload because I want my look and vibe to be as current as possible. One aspect I've really embraced is shooting on location, because a lot of my videos are seasonal. So if I'm going to the beach in the summertime, I'll film there; and when I went to Lake Tahoe for work, I shot a winter-themed video in the snow. It's fun for the videographer in me to get behind the camera and capture a cool scenic shot.

STEP 3: EDITING

HOW I EDIT. I import the video clips to my MacBook Pro laptop, then I use Final Cut Pro to edit the clips. Editing a video can take anywhere from two days to two weeks. There are some videos, like collaborations with other people, that might only take three hours to edit because it's only one shot, one background, and less of a storyline to plot out. But if I want to have intros, effects, music, and a voice-over—which I record on a separate USB mic—that takes time, more than one realizes! Sometimes, I'll hole myself up all day to edit a video, and sometimes I'll work on a video for three weeks, editing a little bit at a time, until it's time to post. If I combine all the editing time together, it can take fifteen hours to edit one eight-minute video.

STEP 4: UPLOADING

WHEN I UPLOAD. Uploading is my favorite part! I like to upload on weekends, because I know my viewers are busy bees during the week. I personally like to binge watch more YouTube videos on weekends (when I actually have some free time!), so I figure that my viewers would appreciate that time, too. But if I upload two videos in one week, I like to space them out by uploading one on Monday and one on Saturday.

MY YOUTUBE SETUP

- I film on a Canon 5D Mark III SLR camera.

- I edit on a MacBook Pro computer.

- I record voice-overs on a Blue Yeti USB microphone; I used to use the Snowball by Blue for a while, which is affordable and also works great.

- I use a heavy-duty but light tripod. I like one that's really sturdy but packs up super-small so I can put it in my suitcase when I travel.

- I have three octagon umbrella lights I use if I need extra lighting, like when I'm shooting in my room. If I'm shooting in the daytime, I always try to get natural light from a window. But if I'm shooting at night or part of the room is dark, I'll use as many octagon lights as I need to make sure there are no weird shadows.

Embracing My Imperfections

When I first got into YouTube, it felt like all the videos I was watching were perfect. So I thought I had to be the same: friendly, but reserved and serious. Because no one else was messing up, I thought I couldn't either. Behind the scenes, I was making lots of mistakes during filming, but I didn't think I should let anyone know that.

But the more comfortable I got in front of the camera, the more often I would do or say goofy things when I messed up. And one day, while I was editing, I just decided to put one of my bloopers in—I think I dropped something and made a funny noise, so I thought I would let people see the real deal.

Viewers really responded to that video, I think, because it showed I'm just human; that I make mistakes like we all do. A lot of viewers commented that they wanted to see more bloopers, that they wanted to get to know me for me—and not just my tutorials or beauty tips. So I started including more of those moments in my videos, including parts where I stumbled over my words, or did something embarrassing, or had to say the same thing over and over like a crazy person to get it right. I put it all in. Viewers loved it, but more importantly, I realized that I loved it. And the more fun I was able to have with it, the more myself I was—on camera and off. I'd always loved showing my goofy side to my friends and family, but I never anticipated showing any of that to my viewers, because I thought those final cuts of my videos were supposed to be perfect. Having the online community accept my silly side made me a little bit braver, and allowed me to start embracing myself wholeheartedly—goofy weirdo and all.

DIY: Create Your Own Ideas Notebook

I keep track of all my creative ideas in a bunch of fun, inspirational notebooks that are small enough to carry around with me. I don't keep them super-professional looking because I feel like creative ideas should be collected in a creative way. One notebook, for example, is gold and reads "Goal Digger" on the front because, as you guys know, I love writing down my goals. And I think it's even cooler if you use notebooks with your own beautiful art or designs on the cover. My favorite way to decorate my notebooks works gold into the mix because who doesn't need a little shimmery inspiration?

WHAT YOU'LL NEED

A black notebook (like a Moleskine, any size), a metallic gold Sharpie, a pencil, paper, and a ruler.

HOW TO MAKE IT

Step 1: Sketch out your design in pencil on paper—because once that metallic pen touches your notebook, there is no going back. I like to play around with a geometric design, like a Navajo-style pattern, or stencil the letters of my favorite word.

Step 2: When your vision is complete, copy your design with your gold Sharpie onto the black notebook. Make sure to use the ruler to create guidelines for your design. If you slip and make a random mark or smear it (like I always do at some point), consider this your design destiny and work it in.

Step 3: Let dry for one hour as you wait for your first creative inspiration to strike!

When My Creativity Is Blocked

I'm such a perfectionist. I used to think being a perfectionist was a good thing, but I've since realized it just means you're never satisfied with what you're doing—and that's usually what leads to a creative block.

I remember a few years ago, a month went by where I couldn't get myself to finish a video. Everything I tried, I thought, "This isn't good enough. No one's going to like it." As the weeks went on, I got in my head even more, thinking, "Well, now it's already been so long since I posted, they're going to expect something really good." And then more time went on and I was like, "Okay, now it's been two months where I haven't put out a video, so it needs to be *amazing*."

SO EMBARRASSING: "I FELL FLAT ON MY FACE"

Falling down in public is a reoccurring pattern for me, though some times are worse than others. One time, I was at a makeup show at a huge community center. I was wearing wedges and a short dress, and I was walking through the middle of the building between all the booths. Suddenly, I hit an uneven part in the flooring, and I tripped and I fell flat on my face! And of course, because I was wearing a short dress, it went flying up when I landed, so people could see everything. Everyone was just staring at me in shock.

For a few seconds, I was just lying there on the ground not sure what to do, so I just got up and . . . walked away. I just completely acted like it didn't happen. I was basically like, "What? No big deal. I meant to do that."

I find the best thing to do in those situations is just laugh about it. Why show people you're bothered? It's already happened, and there's nothing you can do about it, so just go with it and move on. Plus, that day, I had more important things to do and makeup to see!

That happens more often than you'd think. If I go even one week without uploading something, I'll start to beat myself up. And then if I start making something that doesn't feel spectacular enough, the rainstorm of negative thoughts will stop me from finishing it. The only way through a cycle of self-judgment like that is to stop procrastinating and just *do* it. Really, though, I think this kind of doubt and overanalyzing is common for any creative artist; it's part of the process. It's as if my career keeps me on the edge of my seat every day as I take leap after leap without knowing if there is a net at the bottom. Except that I *do* know: My viewers are my net, every time.

My Secrets for Getting Over Procrastination

Every time you get stuck in a rut when you're not being productive, you have two choices: You can procrastinate, make excuses, and create nothing, or you can face what's freezing you, push past it, and create something great. Here's how I get myself moving.

1. *Don't think too far ahead.* Instead of picturing the final result, which can seem very far away or daunting, I just work on what's in front of me in the moment. I'll just edit one clip to get myself going. And once I do, I instantly feel accomplished.

2. *Focus on what you love about your project.* It helps me to remember that I'm working on an idea because I love doing it, not because I *need* to accomplish this goal. Focusing on your enjoyment of the process can give you a jump start on the project itself.

3. *Do it for twenty seconds.* I notice that once I do something for fifteen to twenty seconds, I'm in it. For instance, if I go on the Internet and watch a thirty-second video, suddenly I'm watching all the related videos, and I'm immersed in it. And the next thing I know, my work is done.

4. *Remove distractions.* Distractions have a lot to do with procrastination. For instance: I'll be editing a video that I know needs to be up by a rapidly approaching deadline, yet I'll be distracted by an incoming email that only *seems* urgent in the moment. It's so easy to spend all day long dithering over time-wasters, like checking your Facebook when you know you should be studying, or answering that email you know can sit in your inbox for a few days without any issues. The more distractions you allow yourself, the longer it will take to finish

that big project *you* want to finish. So if you can turn off your Wi-Fi and put away your phone while you work, you'll get more done.

5. *Build a private workstation.* While I work, I sometimes play music on my headphones (if I'm in public) or on my laptop speakers (if I'm home). I find that when I have music playing while I'm editing, it makes me less inclined to click over and watch a non-work video. It's almost like the music is tricking my mind into thinking that there's already something distracting going on!

6. *Decide you'll get it done, even if it's not great.* Whenever I'm in this horrible mindset of doubting myself, I decide I'm going to finish something, no matter how it comes out. I'm like, "Film the video, upload the video." Doing something is always better than doing nothing—and then it's time to move on.

Motavation Inspiration

I'm often asked how I stay motivated—creatively and personally. It's a great question, and I've thought about it a lot because I used to wonder what would happen if the spark inside me fizzled. What if, one day, I just woke up, and I wasn't inspired to do anything? That worry always bubbled under the surface until I realized the solution was in my reach: finding a purpose bigger than myself in whatever it was I was doing.

If you are contributing to your community or helping others in the world, it will light a fire within you that will motivate you in powerful ways. So think about how your strengths can serve a bigger purpose. That could mean learning another language that could help someone on your travels, or it could mean using the knowledge you have to educate people at your local school about an issue that's important to you.

For instance, I worked with UNICEF on their back-to-school campaign to help kids who didn't have basic school supplies. I also worked with PACER's National Bullying Prevention Center, speaking to high schools and middle schools to advocate against bullying. Working with both of those organizations has been a dream come true, because they work toward goals I also am passionate about. By serving them, I get to act on my own passions. The feeling you get when you're using your skills for a greater purpose is the most motivating thing in the world.

MY DIGITAL LIFE

I rely on a lot of apps, software, and tools to bring my creative ideas to life. Here's what I've been using lately.

- I always have my iPhone with me, of course. I use it for everything—calling, texting, taking notes, using social media, ordering food from Postmates, and playing music on Spotify. Literally. Everything.

- Instead of using the regular "Notes" app in my phone, I use an app called Note Lock, so that if someone gets into your phone, they can't see your notes. I have a lot of personal stuff in there, and I like knowing my ideas and thoughts are secure if I ever lose my phone.

- I organize my files into different desktop folders on my computer. I have one folder called "Inspiring Photos," another called "Video Ideas," and one called "Beth Thoughts" where I save my journal writing.

- I use Pinterest. I'll make boards of colors that inspire me, or a board for each season, like a Fall Board or Summer Board. I have some public Pinterest boards, but while I'm still gathering ideas, I keep them private.

- I have an app on my laptop called Pixelmator that I'll use to make collages or some visual ideas boards for my videos.

- I use a website called RealtimeBoard, which is a big online whiteboard that is literally a blank canvas. You can write on it, insert photos, add sticky notes, pin something, or use their premade charts and graphs. But the coolest part is that it's endless, meaning you can grab the page, zoom in and out, move it sideways, and the page goes on and on. This site is the absolute best because it's limitless—just like my ideas.

- I have a few sets of headphones that I use on the go: I have a pair of gold Frends over-ear headphones that I use on long flights to keep the airplane noise out, but those can get really painful and smash your ears over time. So I alternate with the regular Apple headphones or Beats Bluetooth wireless ones.

Dealing with Haters

I've learned a lot about dealing with haters, because I get hateful comments from people around the world—people I've never even met! I'll never forget one of those people, from back in my early days on YouTube.

Every time I posted a new video, this one girl would leave a hate comment on it. I didn't understand why, but she would always find something negative to say, no matter what. I was so confused and, to be honest, really curious: Why was she even on my page and watching my videos if she hated me so much? So I finally messaged her. Because I knew how much other people's negativity had hurt me in the past, I wondered what would happen if I responded in the way she least expected: with positivity.

"I'm sorry that you don't like the videos I'm putting out," I wrote to her, "but thank you for watching. I hope you have a good day." And right away, she sent me a message back where she apologized!

"I'm so sorry," she wrote back. "I'm going through a really rough point in my life, and I've been taking it out on random people." Because I gave her the benefit of the doubt when I reached out to her, she totally changed the way she was talking to me, instantly. And after that, whenever I would get a hate comment from someone else, *she* would start defending me! It really was that instant a turnaround, too. Most of the time, Internet bullies act on impulse; they feel something negative and they act on it immediately—which is why one comment doesn't necessarily represent who someone is as a person as much as their mood in a moment.

That exchange taught me so much: It's easy to write hateful things on the Internet because no one can see you. But I think most of the time, it speaks to the fact that the person leaving hateful comments is going through something, and he or she is taking it out on someone else. It's almost like that person is in such a low place that he or she wants to pull others down there, too. If you can think of it that way—that it's coming from a place of hurt—you'll learn that you should try your best not to take it personally.

Think about it: If you're happy and content with life, the *last* thing you're going to want to do is make someone else feel terrible. That's why I don't normally respond to hate; but if I do, it's only with a positive message.

A Creative Life Is a Happy Life

Once, I was with my friend at the drive-thru of Starbucks. I pulled up to the window and asked about a sandwich I liked.

"Do you guys have more of the bacon Gouda sandwich?" I asked.

"That's a gouda question!" the girl said back.

My friend and I burst out laughing so hard that the girl made, like, five more jokes like that. She basically turned the drive-thru window into her own little comedy show. And I never forgot it. Because she wasn't just doing the job someone had hired her to do; she took that job and made it her own by adding purpose to it—which not only brightened my day, but probably the days of so many other people. And that's what being creative is all about.

Even if you're not working your ideal job, you can still put your full creative energy forward to make the best out of it.

When you're involved in a project and not feeling passionate about it, you can try saying to yourself, "I'm here, right now, for a reason. I just have to figure out why." Maybe it's an important step in your life that you'll understand better later. Maybe you can learn something from it that will help you grow. Or maybe your purpose can be like the purpose of that girl at Starbucks: to brighten the day for the people around you, who will turn around and pass that positive, creative energy on.

Getting
HEALTHY

How I keep my body strong through food and fitness

I've never been one for dieting. Yes, I care about how I look in the mirror, but more important, I care if I'm *healthy* or not. There are some health issues we can't control, but the things we can control—eating fresh and unprocessed food while staying active—can have an incredible effect on our lives. So health is now the number one priority for me, because it has the power to change the only body, and life, I have.

3

Food

{ *I'm embracing the body I have,
and it feels so good.* }

Confession: I Used to Eat So Much Junk Food

I grew up in a small town, and while there were healthy options everywhere, it was easier to eat fast food. I'd hit the drive-thru three to four times a week for a burger and fries, chicken nuggets, or tacos. And if I got French fries, maybe I'd even dip them in a milkshake, because why not? I also ate a lot of meat, sugar, and processed foods. I used to love Hershey's Cookies 'n' Creme chocolate bars, and hot Cheetos. I ate it all. I didn't even know what it meant to eat fresh, natural foods.

The thing was, it never affected my physical appearance; I wasn't gaining weight. So I thought, "I still look good, this is okay." But

while I looked fine, I was always really tired and sluggish throughout the day. So doing some research, I realized that the heavier foods were weighing me down and keeping me from doing the things I wanted to do—and that wasn't okay.

About a year ago, I had one of those "OMG" moments when I realized: *This is the only body I have.* I know. It's so obvious—like *duh.* But at the time, I was like, "Wow, this is the only body I have, and I need my body to take me all the way to the end of my life. And I want to live as long as I can!" For me, that realization was a breakthrough, and I haven't looked back since.

"I Got Your Back, Body."

I used to treat food like it was all about pleasure, instead of thinking of it as the nourishment my body needs to run smoothly. And when I finally realized that I wasn't eating healthy enough foods, I was like, "My body is a *gift* I've been given and I've been treating it so bad. How rude am I?!"

Once I started thinking about the food I was feeding my body and how it affected me internally, it helped change the way I felt about myself externally, too. When I used to go on a "health kick," it was only for vanity, but once I started seeing healthy food as fuel for what I want to accomplish, it changed my whole mindset. My main priority became how I was feeling, and whether or not I had energy, as opposed to how I physically looked to others. I made a vow to my body that I would take better care of it, which is how I started thinking, "Don't worry, body, I got your back."

I Picture Food as Energy

When I was eating junk food, I used to want to take a nap after eating a big meal. I'd just feel tired and want to lie down. But food should energize you, not make you want to sleep! So instead of focusing on portion control or the size of my donut, I focus on not choosing the donut at all. What really helps is to visualize the food I eat as energy. It's like putting gas in a car to make it run—and no body is going to run fast on pizza and potato chips.

About seventy-five percent of what I eat is fruit and vegetables, along with lean protein like fish, supplemented with healthy grains and nuts. I don't eat much meat these days, and I feel so much lighter. I used to worry about overeating, but since I'm mostly eating healthy plants, I don't ever feel bad with how much I eat. Now, when I eat enough, I feel satisfied, full, and ready to go.

Make a Farmer's Market in Your Fridge!

I make plants the centerpiece of my fridge. That way, when I open it, I actually want to eat healthfully. Here's how I prepare my fresh food and make my fridge look like a farmer's market.

Ceramic fruit containers: Instead of storing your fruit in plastic Baggies or containers from the grocery store—they're so not cute—I found these cool containers that *look* like fruit cartons, but they're ceramic. The fruit has to be in a container anyway, so why not a pretty one? I'll wash fruits like blueberries and grapes before I put them in there, so I can just grab them and eat. But softer berries like strawberries and raspberries can get moldy faster if they're wet, so I wait to wash them until before I eat them.

Pre-cut veggies: I buy a lot of pre-cut veggies, like sliced up zucchini, cucumber, and carrots, and I will store them in clear bowls so that when I open the fridge, I can clearly see everything I have to eat, encouraging me to reach for something fresh—and avoid being wasteful.

A cute bowl full of fruit: I will also cut up watermelon or pineapple and put the bite-sized pieces in a glass bowl. Seeing all of it displayed beautifully gives me an appetite for eating healthy.

Drinks in the door: I love my almond milk and coconut milk, but because they're not as pretty as the fresh food I want front and center, I keep them in the door.

MY GIRL POWER IDEA

I want us to change our way of thinking. We need to stop focusing purely on physical appearance and think about the things that matter. So from now on, instead of asking someone else whether he or she lost weight, we should really be asking if he or she is healthy, has been eating well, and has been active. Because we all know that someone can look super-slim and *not* be healthy, right? It's as simple as this: If you take care of yourself, you are beautiful. So let's check in with one another and make sure we're treating ourselves right.

MY DAY OF HEALTHY MEALS

Here's what I tend to choose in a day:

LEMON WATER. I don't drink coffee very often. (Well, I *try* not to drink coffee, but energy emergencies have been known to happen in my world!) Instead, the first thing I do every morning is boil hot water in my electric kettle, squeeze a lemon into it, and garnish it with lemon wedges. Drinking it wakes me up and gives me energy.

BREAKFAST. I try to eat something small before I work out in the morning or else I'll get really sick. I normally do half of a banana, or I'll cut a grapefruit in half and eat it like a bowl of cereal. I always try to choose a food that is raw and natural, rather than something processed. (You can also choose a salad—which I know for some people is crazy before noon, but I've had salads in the morning before!)

SMOOTHIE BREAK. Post-workout, I usually stop at a smoothie place for a green smoothie or an acai bowl topped with berries.

LUNCH. Since I get my fruit in at the start of the day, I try to have a lot of vegetables for lunch, along with some protein. For example, I'll have a piece of either salmon or tuna on a kale salad, with avocado and white beans; or I'll have tofu over broccoli and asparagus with quinoa. Then I'll have broccoli, cauliflower, or roasted carrots on the side. These meals fill me up and give me energy.

HEALTHY DRINK SHOT. Sometimes I'll get a wellness shot on the side after my meal. Typically it's really spicy, with ginger, cayenne, and lemon.

SNACK. I'll bring snacks with me on the go in case I get hungry—usually fruit or some roasted, unsalted almonds.

DINNER. I like to have a good amount of vegetables for dinner, along with a lean protein like salmon or tuna. Grilled salmon with a side of roasted veggies and ahi tuna salads are my go-tos. Other times I'll go straight vegetarian by whipping up some pasta in red sauce with—you guessed it— vegetables on the side, like cauliflower, Brussels sprouts, and broccoli. Lately, I've been trading my pasta for spaghetti squash (when baked, the flesh of this type of squash mimics the shape of angel hair pasta—you can even twirl it around your fork, and eat it with marinara!). Truly, though, my meals vary day to day, guided by what my body craves. If my body talks, I listen!

Beth's Acai Bowl

I love acai bowls. Before I knew what these were, I used to eat a lot of yogurt and eggs for breakfast because we're taught that those are essentially the only breakfast foods besides cereal—but I didn't love them as much as I'm loving acai bowls. Uh, have I mentioned I *love* acai bowls? I'll say it again. I. Love. Acai. Bowls. Seriously, though. Love. Acai. Okay, I'm done.

The acai berry itself (which is pronounced a-sigh-ee) is a little fruit that looks like a purple blueberry. The berries are blended into a puree that mimics ice cream, before being topped with fresh cut fruit, like bananas and strawberries. Sometimes restaurants will add in granola, and occasionally, it will be topped with bee pollen (which might sound crazy, but the taste of the pollen is subtle and it's so good!). An acai bowl is like a dairy-free version of a yogurt bowl. They're super-filling, and every time I eat one I can't believe it's healthy—it's that good. I often grab one on the go, but here's my favorite recipe to make one right at home.

INGREDIENTS

- 1 banana
- 5 strawberries
- 1 (3.5 oz.) package of frozen acai (like the packets from Sambazon)
- handful of ice
- ¼ cup almond milk
- 1 cup kale (I've used spinach, too)
- 1 tsp agave
- ¼ cup granola
- 1 tsp chia seeds
- 1 tbsp shaved coconut

TO MAKE THE ACAI BOWL

Step 1: Slice half of the banana and the strawberries and set aside.

Step 2: Blend the frozen acai, ice, almond milk, the other half of the banana, the kale, and the agave until smooth.

Step 3: Assemble your bowl by pouring the acai blend into the base of the bowl. Place your sliced fruit on top of the acai blend. Top with granola, chia seeds, and shaved coconut. Dig in your spoon and enjoy!

DIY: Decorate Your Own Acai Bowl

What better way to eat your acai creation than from a DIY bowl that is cuter than your average white ceramic dish and cheaper than an Anthro find? Plus, when it comes to healthy eating these days, full meals served in bowls are everywhere: Aside from frozen acai bowls, there are entire restaurants devoted to rice bowls, quinoa bowls, and ramen bowls. Here's how to make a dish to call your own.

WHAT YOU'LL NEED

A wooden bowl, white acrylic paint, Mod Podge, an adhesive stencil (or a few!), and a foam brush.

HOW TO MAKE IT

Step 1: Stick the adhesive stencil to the side of your bowl.

Step 2: Dab white paint onto the stencil with your foam brush. Let it dry. If you can still see the wood through the white paint, do a second coat of paint and let dry.

Step 3: Carefully remove the stencil. You can mix different stencils and freehand some of it for a combination that is uniquely your own.

Step 4: Paint the date and your initials on the bottom of the bowl for a cute, personal touch (and proof that your masterpiece was handmade!).

Step 5: With a clean foam brush, dab the stencil and your signature with a light glaze of Mod Podge and let it dry.

A Crazy Shot of Healthy

Along with eating healthy, I supplement my diet with healthy shots from the health food store, because they give me instant energy. One time, I was going to a meeting and I got super-tired right before, so I took a little health shot after I ate my salad, and I immediately felt so much better.

My favorite shot is the Wellness Shot I get at Earthbar in L.A., with fresh lemon, ginger, oregano oil, garlic extract, and cayenne pepper. The problem is, the shots are so crazy strong, so every time I do one, I feel like I'm going to throw it up! And obviously I don't want to puke in public. (In fact, if you see me in a health food store and I look really weird, I've probably just downed one. So you should definitely stay clear!)

Now I have this routine: I hold my smoothie in one hand and my shot in the other. Then I walk over to the trash can, take the shot, throw the cup away, and then—because the taste is not very pleasant—I literally run out the door (because if I do throw up in public, I'd rather do it on the sidewalk than inside the store!) while taking a sip of my smoothie to try to cover the taste. The shot is so strong that two hours after taking it, I'll still feel my lips stinging.

I'm sure people who see me do this are like, "What is she doing?!" So now you know. I may look weird in the moment, and it may sound crazy on the page, but I always feel better afterward.

To Weigh or Not to Weigh . . . That Is the Question

I used to obsess about weighing myself on the scale. There were time periods when I was feeling insecure about my body and would weigh myself once or even twice a day. Now I don't weigh myself at all. That's partly because I don't own a scale (after moving out of my parents' house, I just haven't bought one yet). But it's also because I haven't cared enough to actually go out and buy one. And I think that's a good thing.

Ever since I started focusing more on my overall fitness and health, I've realized that the most value is in how you feel. If you're gaining a lot of muscle, for instance, you might weigh more, but overall, you'll be healthier. That little, insignificant number on a scale is definitely not indicative of how well you treat your body. And it certainly doesn't dictate how healthy you are. Only your lifestyle, energy, and happiness levels can tell you that.

Kitchen Inspo:
What I Love About My Kitchen

Everyone should have a kitchen that reflects the way he or she cooks and eats. These are the elements that make my kitchen feel like me.

My wood cutting board: I love my cutting board! It's a light wood one that makes for a beautiful background for my fresh veggies and fruits. I want to put a picture of it up on Pinterest every time I cook.

My all-white plates: I have white plates that go with everything and allow the food to be the star. They're like a clean canvas, so I'm more inspired to make colorful, healthy meals.

My gold flatware: No, they're not real gold! But using them makes me feel elegant and sophisticated.

My mug rack: I have a carousel rack that spins. I only put my cute, patterned mugs on there to add a pop of color to my countertop. I make my lemon water in these mugs, and when I run out of clean dishes, I eat my vegan ice cream in them, too.

My flour and sugar containers: I have these really big, white, ceramic flour and sugar containers on my counter, but . . . they're totally empty! I just think they look cool. And they make it look like I bake, which, truthfully, I don't do very often—but you never know: Maybe someday I'll start baking more and need them.

My fruit bowl: Whenever I get apples or bananas, I put them in a bowl on the counter so they're the first thing I see when I'm hungry. If you put your fruit where you can see it, you're more likely to eat it.

My lemon/lime squeezer: One side of it is yellow to squeeze the lemon, and the other side is green to squeeze the lime. It works well and makes for a fun pop of color.

My "Guacamole" Salad

I always thought that to have a good salad, you needed chicken, steak, or cheese. But that's not true! This is one of my favorites because it's like a bowl of guacamole made into a salad, with a dressing that makes it taste like you're at a Mexican fiesta. I have been eating this nonstop.

SALAD INGREDIENTS

- 2 cups fresh spinach, chopped
- 1 Roma tomato, diced
- 1 small avocado, cut into slices or cubes
- 1 can garbanzo beans, rinsed
- ½ red onion, finely chopped
- optional: 10 to 15 corn tortilla chips

DRESSING INGREDIENTS

- ¼ cup grape seed oil
- ¼ cup apple cider vinegar
- 2 tbsp lime juice
- 1 cup fresh cilantro leaves
- 1 strip jalapeño pepper
- ¼ tsp cumin
- salt and pepper, to taste
- red chili flakes

Step 1: In a bowl, combine the spinach, tomato, avocado, garbanzo beans, and red onion.

Step 2: For the dressing, combine the grape seed oil, apple cider vinegar, lime juice, cilantro, jalapeño pepper, cumin, and salt and pepper in a blender or NutriBullet and blend.

Step 3: Pour the dressing over the salad, sprinkle with chili flakes (and tortilla chips, if you're using them), and toss before enjoying.

HOW I... AMP UP MY WATER

Water can be so plain Jane, but it doesn't have to be. I like to switch up my water with different additives (the healthy kind!). These are my favorites:

I INFUSE IT WITH FRUIT OR CITRUS. You already know how I love my lemon water, but sometimes I'll slice up strawberries or drop in whole raspberries. And if I want to relax, I'll slice up cucumbers and let them soak in a pitcher of water overnight, so in the morning my water tastes like it came straight out of a spa. Adding in fruits takes my water from basic to beautiful, and encourages me to drink more of it.

I'LL ADD A FEW CHLOROPHYLL DROPS. Fair warning: It does turn the water that dark shade of green, which, initially, can be really intimidating. In fact, the first time I saw water that looked like that, I wanted to run in the opposite direction. My initial reaction was "I'll take water that looks like water, thankyouverymuch." But then I read how chlorophyll is like the blood of plants and it alkalizes the water, making it even better for you. So I finally tried it—and it isn't that bad! If I want a little boost of energy, I'll add five to ten drops of chlorophyll, which infuses the water with a light grass taste that I barely even notice.

I'LL PUT DIFFERENT POWDERS IN MY WATER. Sometimes I'll add a protein powder or Moon Dust from this L.A. health store Moon Juice, depending on how I want to feel that day.

Getting Body Confident

You know what's messed up? There aren't just clothing trends, there are *body* trends, too, when society implies what our body "should" look like. I get that fashion trends come and go, but having society dictate not only what our bodies should look like, but also how we should treat them so they fluctuate with what's in style . . . that's not okay. Someone shouldn't have to feel pressure to change his or her body because it's considered "cool" to be

a size zero one month and have a curvier butt the next!

A few years ago, it was considered "cool" to have a thigh gap. I have a curvy body that I wasn't yet proud of, so I remember wondering how on earth I could get a gap overnight. And because I didn't have a space between my thighs, I felt so insecure every time I looked in the mirror. And, you know, once you have an insecurity, it can stay with you all day and consume your thoughts. Well, that's how it was for me: I had thigh gaps on the brain.

I started to wonder if I was eating too much and needed to work out more. What a waste of a day—and weeks and months!—spent thinking those things instead of partaking in fun, productive experiences and loving myself. Luckily, I snapped out of it and stopped trying to get a dumb gap. This happened mostly because I gave up on the idea that there's such a thing as one ideal body, and I let go of caring how I was judged for mine. If you have a gap naturally? That's great! If you're curvier? That's great, too! Yes, someone can insult what your body looks like, but if your body is healthy? No one can take that away from you. With that revelation, I reached the highest level of body confidence I've ever had. I'm embracing the body I'm living in. And it feels *so good*.

Eating Goals

When I was growing up, if I wasn't sitting down to dinner with my family, I would eat on the couch or in bed. But I would eat mindlessly, paying almost no attention to what I was putting in my mouth. Usually, they weren't even full meals, so I would end up still hungry.

Now I try to really engage with the food I'm eating without any distractions—you know, really taste my meal and experience all five senses working in tandem. Instead of liking thirty-two photos of kittens on Instagram while I eat, or watching a bunch of YouTube videos while I eat, I'm trying to actually just, you know . . . eat.

It's hard for me, because it's such a social media world and we're always on our phones and computers. (I'm sure I'm not the only one, and hey, it's my job!) But I've found that I'm way more satisfied and stay full for longer when I actually sit there and give my meal the attention it deserves.

A Berry Beautiful Idea: Make Your Own Lip Stains

I sometimes use natural foods as vibrant lip stains. Here are three of my favorites from good ol' Mother Nature, followed by instructions on how to turn them into a stain for naturally luscious lips.

Acai berries make really good lip stains (as if I couldn't love 'em more!). I learned this while I was in Hawaii with my friend. I had just eaten my acai bowl when she saw my lips and said, "Oh my god, I *love* that color!" My lips were a dark shade of purple—and it was from the acai! I just blended it in and it looked beautiful. About one tablespoon of frozen acai berries should be enough to make your stain.

Beets are good for that, too. You'll want to cut up a lipstick-sized piece from a raw beet to make your stain. You can wear a glove for this one if you want, as you may dye your fingers with it at the same time—it can take a bit of scrubbing to rid your fingers of the tint!

Raspberries are the simplest way to get a punchy pink shade on your lips. About five fresh berries should get you a good dose of juice.

HOW TO MAKE IT

What You'll Need: A fruit/vegetable, organic brown sugar, rubber spatula, Vaseline, small glass or ceramic container, and a lip brush.

Step 1: Blend your fruit/vegetable until it is smooth. Add one teaspoon of organic brown sugar.

Step 2: In a bowl, use a rubber spatula to mix your product with around one teaspoon of Vaseline—use a little more or less fruit/vegetable, depending on how vibrant you want your hue.

Step 3: Scrape your blend into a small container, and store in the refrigerator. When you're ready to use it, dip a lip brush into your blend and apply to your lips.

Bethany's Brussels

If I could have one food for the rest of my life, it'd be Brussels sprouts. It's so weird, but I just love them. This is my favorite way to cook them up.

INGREDIENTS

- **1 bag of Brussels sprouts, with the ends chopped off and sliced in half lengthwise (or purchase them pre-cut)**
- **2 tbsp olive oil**
- **salt and pepper, to taste**
- **1 tbsp vinegar**
- **2 lemons, juiced**

TO MAKE THE SPROUTS

Step 1: Preheat the oven to 350°F.

Step 2: Wash the Brussels sprouts, dry them off, and put them in a big bowl. Drizzle them with the olive oil and season with salt and pepper. Toss them around in a bowl to coat the sprouts.

Step 3: Lay the sprouts on a baking sheet and bake for forty minutes. I'll check on them after about twenty minutes to see how it's going and flip them over.

Step 4: Toss them in the bowl again, this time with the vinegar and lemon juice.

Step 5: Eat! Trust me, you guys, they're *so* good.

4

Fitness

{ All it takes to keep your body moving . . . is to move it! }

Hey Body, Move It!

I was really active as a kid, since I wasn't constantly glued to an iPhone or tablet. I was going outside, running down the trails by the cows, playing with my friends, and practicing cheer. But once I got into YouTube and social media, I basically stopped moving. Honestly, I feel like our entire generation stopped moving right along with me—investing time and energy into making the Internet a big part of your day-to-day can lead to such a sedentary lifestyle. And the less I moved, the more tired I was. This past year, I've realized that keeping your body in motion is just as important as feeding it healthy food.

Every morning now, I wake up, blast music, and dance around before I go work out. If there's a day when I don't make it to the gym, I make it a point to turn up music and dance around my room for a longer amount of time. And if I'm ever feeling down or unenergized, I'll just raise my hands up above my head and jump up and down in one spot. I know. It's weird. But it really does help, because you're engaging your whole body all at once.

Here's the thing: *Anyone* can get his or her body moving. It's easy to get caught up in excuses, but not having a gym membership, or the time, or the right equipment is not a solid reason to avoid keeping active. And we know it. Because, literally, all it takes to keep your body moving . . . is to move it! Physical motion completely changes how you live, feel, and breathe—so I honor myself by honoring my body.

My Secret to a Good Mood

Your mental state depends a lot on what you're doing physically. Think about it: If you're lying down, sluggish and not moving, or just standing still and hunched over, it's like you're sending a message to your body that you're defeated—your endorphins aren't flowing, your energy levels aren't rising. But if you're at a concert and you like the music, you physically might be jumping up and down and waving your arms. So when you're doing that at home, away from a concert, it's like you're tricking yourself by saying, "Body, how happy are we?!" In fact, it's not even a trick: Increased physical motion like jumping, dancing, and exercising releases endorphins, increases adrenaline, and may even increase the brain's happiness neurotransmitter serotonin. (For real, you guys, I researched it!)

So I use that science to my advantage: If I want to be in a better mood, I persuade my mind that I'm energized and happy by moving my body. If I move it and shake it and dance with it, I literally can't help but be in a better mood.

RANDOM ME FACT: I LOVE SWEATING

Sweating during a workout is your body responding to effort; it's proof that what you're doing is working. I actually get a little discouraged when I don't sweat during a workout, because I feel like I didn't push myself hard enough! One of the reasons I love to work out early in the morning is because it gives me time to shower before I get ready for work. When I start my day with a good sweat, it usually turns out to be a good day.

My 5 Go-To Workouts

Basically, I do one of these workouts, five days a week.

WORKOUT 1

Circuit training or Pilates with my trainer: I like getting outdoors in the morning to meet up with my trainer. I work out with her for an hour, and we'll switch it up: Some days, we'll do boxing, which takes so much out of you because you're working every part of your body (I usually can't feel my arms the day after), and other days we'll do Pilates, but most of the time we do combinations of cardio and strength exercises in sets of twenty. First, we'll do twenty jumping jacks, then twenty jumps with a jump rope, followed by twenty squats, and end the circuit with twenty burpees (which, can we agree, is the weirdest name for a move ever? The first time I heard it, I thought it was something you'd buy for a baby . . .) Anyway, with all of these workouts, she mixes it up so I'm never bored.

WORKOUT 2

Cycling class: Sometimes I'll do a fifty-minute cycling class with a friend. It's basically like working out in a nightclub—I'll never say no to sweating to loud music!

WORKOUT 3

Aerial class: Aerial training class lasts for an hour. And sometimes, I'll double up in one day by working out in the morning, and then attending an aerial class before a meeting.

WORKOUT 4

Treadmill + planks: If I'm traveling, I'll jump on the treadmill at the hotel gym—but instead of running, I do incline walking. I just make sure the incline is high enough that I feel the burn in my legs and it becomes a struggle to keep up the pace (I know, sounds so fun!). I'll incline walk for thirty to forty minutes—or sometimes for an hour and a half—if you alternate the incline periodically, it feels like going on a difficult hike. Before and after, I'll do a plank for a minute or two.

WORKOUT 5

A workout per song: Sometimes, I find it hard to keep track of how many reps of a certain move I've done, because I'm focusing so much on what my body's feeling (or, let's be real, singing along to Beyoncé in my head). So I'll sometimes do a circuit training workout where I use my music to guide me: I'll plank for one song, jump rope for another, do mountain climbers for the next song, and do reverse crunches for another song. I'll keep that rhythm up for about an hour.

I Go All Out with My Workout Wear

Workout clothes make me feel really happy—aside from the fact that they complement the body well, workout clothes are not constrictive; they're ready for whatever you feel like doing in the moment. So if I'm wearing yoga pants and running shoes, I can do flips down the street if I want to! Although, in reality, I'll just be more comfortable walking down the street to get my smoothie.

I have fun choosing my workout wear. Because if I get a new sports bra or cool yoga pants, I'm way more excited to work out so I can wear them.

I tend to choose items that each have a distinctively unique element—like a nylon cutout or a section with a textured eyelet fabric. In fact, I had one pair of yoga pants with cutouts all over them, and you could see some skin through them. I got tons of compliments on those particular ones. (And then I lost them. *So* me. I still miss them every day—they were so cool!)

I color coordinate my outfits, too. For example, I might wear a hot-pink, long-sleeve neon shirt with my hot-pink and orange-neon running shoes and black yoga pants. Or, I'll wear those black yoga pants with black Nikes for a streamlined look. (Generally, I'm a black yoga pants girl. Every once in a while I'll wear yoga pants with a print, but they won't be "disco galaxy cats in space" pants. Does someone even make those? You know, I bet they do. And power to those people. I just probably won't be wearing them!)

My 2 Workout Styles

I usually go for one of two vibes when choosing my workout apparel, depending on what I'll be doing that day:

WORKOUT STYLE #1: TOUGH

When I'm doing hardcore moves at the gym or with my trainer, I want workout gear that helps me feel strong and empowered.

- Yoga pants. I like Lululemon's thick, black, high-waisted yoga pants that can handle a tough workout and that also go all the way down to the ankle. (I feel like the cropped ones make me look shorter.) Plus, if I have somewhere to go after working out, I can just throw on a chic oversized shirt or a sweater.

- A bright sports bra. The one from Victoria's Secret is my go-to because it's thick (for more support) and comes in fun colors.

- T-shirt or tank. I normally wear a T-shirt or tank top over my sports bra— but

I always make sure it's made of really lightweight material if I know I'm in for a particularly intense workout.

- Colorful sneakers. I have a few pairs in different colors, and I'll coordinate them to my outfit.

- A zip-up sweater. If I'm working out in the morning and it's still chilly outside, I'll throw on my black Nike zip-up sweater to keep me warm and wick away sweat.

WORKOUT STYLE #2: GRACEFUL

When I'm doing yoga, Pilates, or aerial, I tend to wear looser, flowier, ethereal pieces that make me feel more feminine.

- Yoga pants. Again, I wear the high-waisted ones that go down to the ankle, which go from the gym to the yoga studio with ease.

- Loose shirts. I choose shirts I can move in when I do aerial. One of my favorites is a loose, gray T-shirt with wider sleeves. Bonus points if you find shirts made out of the softest material around!

- Bare feet. For aerial and yoga, I'm barefoot . . . so I just make sure I have a cute pedicure.

My Power Bun

When I was on *Dancing with the Stars*, I was rehearsing a lot with my hair down. Then one day, I put it in a tight, low bun with a middle part, and something happened. Suddenly, I felt like a real, bona fide dancer. That tiny change to my hairstyle completely altered my mental state, and I quickly improved during that practice session. (More on that crazy show experience in a minute!)

So that's one of my workout secrets now: putting my hair in a tight bun. I feel like it makes me look polished, clean, strong, and in control—and somehow helps me channel my inner strength. Here's how I pull mine together.

Step 1: I part my hair straight down the middle with my fingers.

Step 2: I pull both sides back, grab it into a ponytail, and tie with a hair band.

Step 3: After tying it with a band, I wrap my hair around itself into a bun.

Step 4: I tie a hair band around the bun.

Step 5: If you need to, you can put in bobby pins to hold it tighter. I don't do this a lot, but I should because my bun always ends up falling out halfway through my workout!

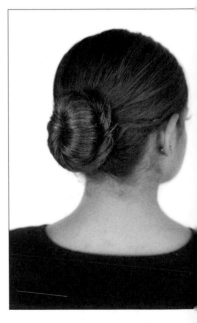

My Workout Makeup

I sometimes apply makeup before a workout—I know, I know, some people just don't get it. But I say, do what you want! Do what makes you feel good. And what makes me feel good is putting on makeup before some of my lighter workouts. It gives me an energy boost, and I feel a little more awake.

If I work out with my trainer and I know it's going to be intense and I'll be sweating it out, I usually don't take the time to put any on. But if I'm doing yoga, aerial, or a lighter Pilates workout, I'll massage a little tinted moisturizer all over my face, and use a little concealer where I feel is necessary. I'll also touch up my eyebrows with a brow pencil before topping off my face with a sweep of translucent powder. I'll finish the look off with a light pink or peach lip balm or gloss. And then, even before I work out, I'm glowing!

A PERFECT HEALTHY DAY

I don't have a day exactly like this every day, but I aim for it as often as possible.

6:00 AM: Wake up. Dance around!

6:30 AM: Eat some fruit before my workout.

7:00–8:00 AM: Work out for an hour.

8:30 AM: Shower off the sweat, get dressed, and do my hair and makeup.

10:00 AM: Make a smoothie or pick up an acai bowl.

10:30 AM: Go to work meetings.

11:30 AM–2:00 PM: Work on YouTube and other career-related opportunities.

2:00 PM: Lunch while working, with protein, grains, and lots of veggies.

2:30 PM: Down a healthy juice shot.

2:30 PM–5:30 PM: Work more (as Rihanna says: *work work work work work work . . .*).

5:30 PM: Hike with friends.

7:00 PM: Have dinner.

7:30 PM: Stretch with foam rollers.

8:00 PM: Make some herbal tea.

8:45 PM: Zone out with a bubble bath and a book.

10:00 PM: Climb into my comfy bed for eight hours of restful sleep.

SO EMBARRASSING: "MY FIRST SOULCYCLE CLASS WAS MORTIFYING!"

The first time I went to SoulCycle, I went alone. Little did I know what a mistake that would be!

First, I got there five minutes late. I didn't think that was a big deal, but it meant that when I walked in, the lights were already off, so I couldn't find my bike in the dark room. While everyone was pedaling, I had to ask the instructor if she could lead me to my bike. Then she looked down at my feet.

"You need the shoes," she said. (I'm not even sure how she could see my shoes, it was so dark in there.)

"What do you mean?" I asked. "These are my Nikes, they're my workout shoes." I was so confused, thinking, "Was I supposed to wear Adidas or something?"

"No," she said, "you need the special shoes with the clips on the bottom."

So I ran out of the room, rented a pair of shoes, and then clomped back in on the special clip-bottomed ones.

By then, it was ten minutes into the class. The woman clipped me in, and suddenly I started to feel panicky, thinking, "I can't get out of these even if I wanted to."

I tried to keep up with the class, but I was in a class with no beginners, so every single person knew what they were doing, while I was in the back, sweating and trying to keep up.

Because I was so hot, I grabbed my water bottle and took a drink of water, but then, because it was so dark and I couldn't see anything, I had trouble getting it back in the cup holder. So I placed it where I thought it went . . . and my water bottle fell to the floor. So then I started panicking again because I was thinking, "I'm gonna vomit if I don't drink water." I reached down again and again, trying to get my water off the floor, but I couldn't reach it—and I couldn't get out of the pedals to get it, either! So instead, I grabbed my towel to mop up my sweat. Then I dropped that on the floor accidentally, too.

Toward the end of the class, we finally got to the point where everyone held weights for the toning exercises—but I didn't know the weights were on the back of the bikes.

"Excuse me!" I shouted to the instructor. "I don't have any weights!"

I guess the girl in front of me just wanted me to be quiet, so she gave me the weights from her bike to use. Except that as soon as we were finished with the weight exercises, I didn't know where to put them! I watched and saw that other people were putting them behind the bikes, so I tried to do the same. But of course I didn't realize each bike already *had* weights back there, so when I tried to place my new pair back there, they didn't fit and fell so hard to the ground, they rolled into the girl's bike next to me! This, mind you, is as the music's going down, and you just heard this huge bang from my side of the room, which sounded like I'd just gotten angry and thrown the weights aside. So *everyone* was staring at me.

Finally, at the very end, everyone got off the bike to stretch, right? Well I didn't know how to get off the bike, so I just had to sit on it, super-awkwardly, and pretend I meant to stay there—until the instructor finally came over and helped me get off.

The whole class was just so embarrassing! Because it wasn't one thing that happened, it was literally one thing *every ten minutes*. If I'd gone with a friend, it would have been easier than going alone. So you'd think that when I took my sister for the first time, I'd have been helpful. But instead, I laughed and said, "You have to figure it all out on your own!"

DIY Healthy Inspo:
Make an Inspirational Quote Wall

Over the years, I've made what I call "gallery walls" to inspire me to reach for my goals every day—and when I'm down about dragging myself to the gym, an encouraging (and pretty!) pick-me-up is usually just what I need. I like to print cool quotes in nice fonts and put them in matching white frames. It's always fun to add some images into the mix—and voilà: inspiration that's also a piece of art!

WHAT YOU'LL NEED

White frames in varying sizes and shapes (or black and white frames in the same shape), paper, nails or picture hangers, and a hammer. In addition, get one decor item, like a gold animal head or a letter of your first initial that lights up.

HOW TO MAKE IT

Step 1: Look up quotes that inspire you about health and happiness, as well as pretty nature photographs or graphics that make you happy.

Step 2: Type the quotes into your computer and mix up the fonts, font sizes, and colors. I like a nice watercolor font that looks like it was painted. (I get my fonts from dafont.com, which is one of my favorite websites. It's free, full of unique typefaces, and fun to say, obviously.) Print out your quotes.

Step 3: Then, print out some of the photos you like. If you're feeling extra creative,

you can layer a quote onto one of the photos, or collage a few photos into one frame.

Step 4: Frame the images.

Step 5: Once all of the photos and quotes are framed, lay them down on the floor and fiddle with the arrangement until you come up with the best layout.

Step 6: Hang them on your wall, placing your one random decor item into the mix to break up the frames and add to the look. Become inspired!

My Tricks for Motavating My Butt Out of Bed

Trust me, there are plenty of days I don't want to work out. So I have some tricks that force me to get out of bed and into motion.

1. *I schedule super-early workouts.* I'll schedule a workout appointment at 7 am, which means I need to leave my apartment around 6:30 am, which means I need to wake up at 6 am to keep my scheduled appointment, whether I want to or not.

2. *I get someone else involved.* If I'm working out alone, I can easily convince myself to skip a day . . . or three. But if someone is waiting for me who will be upset if I'm not there? It motivates me. So I'll schedule an appointment with my trainer or sign up for a class with a friend who can be my workout buddy.

3. *I picture how accomplished I'll feel later.* On days I don't want to wake up, I have a decision to make: "Do I want to start making my good decisions now, or do I want to sleep in, feel gross later, and have to fix it?" Working out early starts a positive momentum for my whole day. It's like, "Now that I've started, I can't stop." Plus, when I work out in the morning, my day is so much longer; after a 6 am wake-up call, 10 am feels like my usual 1 pm if I wake up at 9 am (math, people).

4. *I force myself out of bed for ten minutes.* Once you've been out of bed for ten minutes, it's actually tough to get back *in* bed, because you're in the wake-up zone. So I tell myself, "Girl, you *know* this is going to be rough, but only the first ten minutes will be torture." So as soon as my alarm goes off, I get up and go to the bathroom to pee, or the kitchen to get a piece of fruit because I'm hungry. All you need is one thing to make you get out of bed, and then you're up. You could also put your iPhone across the room so that you have to get up to turn it off—though if I did that, I wouldn't hear it. I sometimes have to put my phone *on* my bed with me and set ten different alarms, two-to-five minutes apart, to be sure one of them actually wakes me up. I'm not kidding! Separating from my phone is just too risky for me. I sleep *deep*, you guys.

5. *I buy new workout wear.* I have a big collection of fun-colored gear that helps me get motivated in the morning. Because if I know I have a cute outfit waiting for me, I'll be excited to wake up and wear it. It's like fitness Christmas.

Dancing into a Healthy Life

I started getting really interested in my health when I was cast on *Dancing with the Stars*. And the way I was approached by the network was so cool. One of the producers had a daughter who watched my videos, and she told her mom that she thought I'd be a great candidate for the show. When I finally met Deena's daughter, I was like, "It's so good to meet you, thanks for telling your mom!"

When they first asked me, I wasn't ready to compete yet. I just wasn't ready to step out of my comfort zone and try something so new.

Thinking back on it, my ego really got in the way of my decision and eventually my performance. I worried I would mess up because dancing was so different from what I was used to—and if I did mess up, I wouldn't have control over how viewers saw me, as I did on my YouTube channel. In fact, I was so focused on what people would think of me that I forgot there was an entire other *show* happening. Deep down, though, I really wanted to do it. I'd done dance competitions when I was twelve or thirteen, and I always felt a pull to dance again. So as

RANDOM ME FACT: I CAN BE A TOTAL KLUTZ

Don't be surprised at how many stories I'm telling where I fall on my face or break something. For some reason, I'm always hurting myself. I run into things a lot, and I'm always stubbing my toe randomly. Sometimes I'll even have a cut on my hand and I literally don't know how it happened. It doesn't surprise me anymore because when I was younger, I was always falling and had scuffed-up, bloody knees. I basically had three Band-Aids on both my knees at all times for half of my childhood. As I got older, I traded scraped knees for hot glue gun burns, but still—I just let it happen!

soon as I caught myself thinking that I kind of, sort of wanted to (*maybe* . . .) try it out, I focused on *that* feeling more. And even though I was still scared, I took the leap anyway, and agreed to compete on the show. Little did I know that I would come to have the best partner ever.

Behind the Scenes: Meeting Derek Hough

I wanted Derek to be my partner, but of course you don't get to pick. At one point, they were interviewing me while I had the webcam on my laptop open; I was shooting a video to document the experience. The next thing I knew, I saw Derek in my webcam, coming in the door behind me, and I yelled, "Derek!!" I was so excited it was almost awkward (which is pretty much normal for me!).

I learned so much more than just dance from Derek. I mean, I felt like a lost puppy going into this, and when I got nervous, he was always there for me. A few times, I felt so beaten up by the competition, so emotionally drained, and even physically sick. Rather than letting me sit there, feeling sorry for myself, he'd say, "How can we handle it? How can we take action?" I learned a lot about inner strength from him. The only time he wasn't calm, cool, and collected was for one dance we did as a tribute to Gene Kelly, *Singin' in the Rain*—that's essentially his *favorite* person ever, so he was super-anxious about the whole thing.

What's funny is that Derek is ten years older than me, but sometimes I feel like he's younger! He just has a very childlike spirit. When we were practicing, he would make a lot of sound effects—my favorite was when he'd speak in weird voices or he'd make panting noises as if he was a dog when he was thinking hard about a move in the choreography. It's rare to see someone so in touch with the child within himself—and yet when he's focused, he's one hundred percent on, ready, and down to do the work that needs to be done.

I cherish our friendship now. It's like friendship on steroids. You know when you've known someone for so long—like, ten years—that you go through these emotional situations that bring you closer? In the *Dancing* competition, we experienced those same things but in a matter of three months, so it feels like Derek and I have been friends for ten years. Close friends with whom you share such a strong bond come few and far between, and so I could not be more thankful for stepping out of my shell and competing on the show!

Dancing: Harder Than It Looks

A few days before my first episode of *Dancing with the Stars*, I was doing a jive move wrong for too long and didn't know it, until I felt this weird discomfort in my foot. The rest of my body was in pain from all the dancing, so I didn't really notice it, and didn't see a doctor right away. I just started wrapping it and doing ice baths. (You know me, always trying to DIY everything!) But over the course of the week, the pain got really bad, and I finally went to the doctor. Apparently, I'd fractured my ankle!

Normally when you fracture your ankle, they tell you to get off it, but I couldn't—I wasn't about to back out of the competition, no way! So I kept going. It was funny, though, because I'd be in these elaborate rhinestone costumes . . . with a wrap around my ankle. But I decided to just own it. Everything they put you in is so over-the-top anyway: I always had two sets of false eyelashes and tons of makeup on—you could take a knife and scoop it off. I didn't even recognize myself! And then, of course, when I eventually saw myself on TV, I was like, "Oh, I look so natural. They could have put on even more."

Anyway, the show was one of the most stressful things I've ever done in my life. Rehearsals are eight hours each day (on a typical day, I went to the dance studio at noon and didn't leave until 10 pm). Then we'd have a show Monday, and then—Boom!—right after the show, we were back in the rehearsal studio for five days to prepare for next week's episode.

I was so out of my element. I had danced a little bit in the past, but *nothing* prepared me for that show. None of the contestants are professional dancers, but we're still expected to perform like we are. Plus, as I mentioned, I'm so used to being on YouTube, where you can mess up and edit as you need to. But when you're in front of a live audience and millions of people are watching at home? It's terrifying.

It was also so, so hard to get the dance moves right. So many times during the competition, I'd tell myself, "I can't do that move," because I didn't think I could. But the more I practiced, the more moves I nailed. So as we went on, I started telling myself, "I *can* do that move, I *will* do that move." And then, lo and behold, I'd be able to master it in a shorter time than I would have otherwise. It helped me recognize the power I actually held, and the ability I had to put my mind to something new and get it done. Time and time again, I would surprise myself by crossing a threshold I didn't know I could.

DIY: Build a Workout Beauty Survival Kit

If I don't have time to shower after a workout, I'll bring a survival bag with me for much-needed touchups.

WHAT YOU'LL NEED

A slim, zippered pouch that is big enough to hold these items, but small and flat enough to drop into your purse.

HOW TO MAKE IT

Fill your bag with these items:

Dry shampoo spray. I get the mini bottles of Big Sexy Hair or Drybar dry shampoo that I can put in my purse. I spray it in my roots, massage it in to get rid of the oil, and use it as hairspray sometimes. You can also use baby powder if you prefer. In either case, just make sure to fully work it into your hair: If you're a brunette, dry shampoo can leave light gray traces behind if you don't work it through properly!

A tiny little comb. When your hair's greasy, it gets flat, so I'll use a small comb to tease my hair a little in the front of my crown, right on the top of my head.

A travel-sized deodorant. Just because I don't shower doesn't mean I don't want to smell good!

Hair ties. If my hair is sweaty or frizzy and doesn't look good down no matter what I do, I'll tease it, spray some dry shampoo, and put it up in a high ponytail.

Band-Aids. I'm always hurting myself or stubbing my toe, especially if I'm working out. So if you're like me, this will come in handy for you, too.

DON'T JUST WATCH TV

Sometimes I have nights where I watch movies or a bunch of TV shows in a row. But I try to remind myself there are things I can do instead of just sitting there, staring at a box. I'm so not into the "Couch Potato" thing; I prefer feeling more like a fresh Couch Carrot. These moves aren't about working out per se, but, rather, keeping my body moving in some small way.

I STRETCH. I'll get in a butterfly stretch, or the lotus position where your legs are crossed and the bottoms of your feet are sitting on your thighs.

I HAVE FOAM ROLLERS, to smooth out what's been hurting if I'm working out a lot.

I'LL KINDA DO SPLITS . . . but I can't really do those yet! I used to be able to do a full split when I was younger, so I'm trying to get back to that point.

I'LL DO SQUATS. As soon as I press play on Netflix, I'll start doing them. I focus on my form and keep doing them until it gets too difficult to do a single one more. (I do squats when I'm blow-drying my hair, too—but not so many that I start to sweat.)

I'm Learning to Be Vulnerable

On the outside, I feel like I clicked with the rest of the cast members on *Dancing with the Stars*. Alfonso Ribeiro, who won, was essentially the stage uncle for everyone, and we all went to him for emotional advice. Janel Parrish from *Pretty Little Liars* was on my season, and we bonded over how many bruises we were getting (I had more, as usual); we're still close friends today. Jonathan Bennett from *Mean Girls* was awesome, too. What I loved most about him was how genuinely happy he was for the experience, despite the overwhelming stress. He was stoked for every dance, and lived for every note he got from the judges, which is why I'm still friends with him now.

On the inside, though, I struggled. The thing was, I had to be really vulnerable on the show while I danced and talked about my personal life on screen, and that was hard for me, because I hate being vulnerable! So I didn't open up very much. And looking back on it, I should have thrown my real self into my on-air interviews a lot more. I should have been like, "Here's the real deal me" and admitted how freaked out I was. Instead, I internalized everything.

And here is the real deal with me: I feel everything *so* deeply—either I love something or it's nonexistent to me. And when I was doing this competition, I was *in* it! It meant the world to me, so I was throwing everything I had into practice and my performances. But on the surface, I looked so chill—too chill, apparently. (Kind of like my day interviewing President Obama at the White House.) Because even though in my mind I was going crazy, it looked like I didn't care, that I didn't want to win. But I absolutely, positively did!

I was really emotional when we got eliminated fourth from the end, but it wasn't because we lost; it was more because such an amazing journey was coming to an end. And the last freestyle dance we did was the best, because I could just relax and have fun. If I ever did this or something like it again, I'd try to get out of my head, show my emotions, and enjoy the experience by being one hundred percent me.

FUN FITNESS: GO SALSA DANCING!

I am trying to keep dance a part of my life no matter what, whether I'm going to a dance class or doing some hip-hop moves around my living room by myself. I don't even need the appropriate genre of music for my moves; I'll salsa to Justin Bieber and I'll have fun while doing it!

Another thing you can do is go to a salsa night at a local dance studio—either on a date or with your girlfriends. With a guy, dancing builds a trust because there's something so intimate about being physically close to someone else and trusting him enough to follow his lead. And if you go with your girlfriends, you get to bond, let loose, and have fun while also trying something new. (And remember what happened when I went to my first spin class alone? Yeah, I didn't want to do that again, so I go armed with friends whenever I can!) Either way, you meet so many great people—including dancers who really know how to salsa, doing flips and dips and spins. Being in that energy makes you feel powerful, so that by the time you step off of the dance floor and into your next activity, you can accomplish anything you try.

Bring on the Next Challenge!

On the show, there was something happening every minute of the day—whether it was rehearsal, interviews, press events, or the shows—and in between, I also had to squeeze in my YouTube stuff. Somehow, though, I got it all done, as if there were twice as many minutes in a day. Instead of sitting down and watching TV for an hour, I was *living*. I was using my body to its full capacity and making the most of every moment.

After the show ended, I cherished my time like I never had before and continued making the most out of it. I started painting and taking singing lessons; anytime I had a free hour, I'd think something like "Maybe I can start learning a new language or trying a new sport for the first time," because nothing felt off-limits. There are so many more minutes in a day than you think, so instead of wasting time on your phone or tablet, take advantage of them!

My Favorite (Ouch!) Workout Move: Planks

When I used to do planks, I'd think, "Oh this is so easy." Apparently . . . I was doing them wrong. When I started planking the proper way, I was think-screaming, "Agghhhh!" If you do it right, it works your arms, legs, abs, *everything*. And you can do it everywhere—no excuses. Here are the steps I follow to achieve a perfect, burning, tortuous plank (I know, I make it sound so fun!):

Step 1: Get on your elbows and balance on your toes with your feet hip-width apart.

Step 2: Make sure your back is even and really flat, and you're scooping up into your abs—imagine trying to touch your belly button to your spine. (Weird, I know, but if you think about this image while you're planking, you'll get it right.)

Step 3: Put as much weight on your arms as you do on your legs. I used to push my body backwards, but you should be creating even tension in your whole body so you're feeling it in your arms, abs, and legs.

How long to do it: I'll set a timer and do a plank for one to two minutes. In some cases, I'll play a song and be like, "Okay, I have to hold this pose throughout the whole song." Then, when it's done, I feel good that I've finished a tough plank *and* got to listen to my jam.

MY LOVE-YOUR-BODY THEORY

Before I started taking aerial classes, I used to think it looked so easy. The aerial performers were just hanging there, right? Even *kids* do that. (I guess this "Looks so easy" thing is a theme for me!) Oh, no. It's hard. It's *so* hard, I almost had my first aerial fall the other day. It happened while I was holding on to the fabric and trying to reach up to a higher spot. I thought I could just let go, but, you know . . . *gravity*. That darn thing is always getting in the way! I wasn't that high off the ground, but the weight of my body pulled me down toward the floor—fast—and my coach had to catch me. That was the first time I realized I could actually fall off and hurt myself (duh, I know), and since then I've pushed my body even more to stay safe.

The coolest thing about aerial, though, is that every muscle is activated the whole time—even your fingers. So, mentally, you really connect to your body and you feel the full power your body holds.

I have a theory now: If you include activities in your life that work your *whole* body—whether it's yoga, aerial, rock climbing, or dancing—you'll feel gratitude for what your body is capable of—and when you realize how much you need all your muscles for everything you do, you will be proud of the strong body you have.

Getting
GORGEOUS

*How I play up my personal
clothing and makeup style*

We tell our stories through our personal style and beauty. It's a form of self-expression. And what's cool is that no one else decides what we choose to wear or how we do our makeup and hair. It's all up to us, and it's just so very personal. And honestly, my style can be summed up in just a few words: I love to feel like *me*.

5

Style

Trends aren't set rules. They're simply suggestions.

My Funny Style Fails

When I was ten or eleven, I had a very distinct style: I would only wear bright colors, which was what I considered "in fashion." Then, when I was thirteen, I realized you could mix patterns (like florals and stripes) and textures (like denim and leather). But I got so excited about mixing things that I went overboard and mixed everything! I look back and I'm like, "Oh my god, what was I thinking?!"

I'll never forget one really out-there outfit I wore (and I'm so sorry I don't have a photo of it!). It was a cropped bulky sweater that I wore over a weird, loose, tank top–type shirt, along with baggy jeans and big loose socks that were practically like leg warmers. I was trying to be "winter fashionable," but it totally backfired and I just looked "winter crazy person." Basically, I tried so hard to be fashionable that I overdid it by over-layering and mixing too many trends at once. While I do wonder what I was thinking when I look back at some of my former fashion misses, the truth is, there's no such thing as bad fashion, because each outfit tells our story at that time. Granted, I was telling so many over-the-top "stories," in those years, my style ended up swinging the other way.

Now I prefer simplicity, and I balance things in a way that works for me. For instance, I still love statement pieces, but I won't wear fifteen at once. Sure, I still have bad days while trying to figure out my own style. But I'm having more fun with it, and taking inspiration from women I see who wear what they like with confidence; women who just *own* it.

Trends Are for Setting

When I was clueless about style, I would go to the mall and buy the entire outfit that was on a mannequin, figuring that if they put that outfit in a window, it *must* be good! I didn't realize at the time that what looks good on a stick-thin plastic figure wouldn't necessarily look good on me. Or that sometimes they're just having fun with the mannequins—like how Forever 21 might go crazy with the mixing on the store model, but you wouldn't wear the entire outfit out in public (although if you choose to rock that look, more power to you).

Eventually, I stopped looking at mannequins and trends and started developing my own style. After all, trends aren't set rules; they're simply suggestions. I started shopping based on my body and what I liked—and suddenly every day felt like an opportunity to express myself. I think my style's gotten simpler, but it feels just as experimental as it did back in the day.

Sometimes I feel the most beautiful in sweatpants, because that's *my* definition of what's cute. Your definition of stylish might be different from mine, but that's what makes it so fun—and what can make each of us so fearless in our own way.

WHERE I GET MY STYLE IDEAS

I may not follow *all* the trends anymore, but I do get inspired by . . .

STYLISH WOMEN. I've always loved Lauren Conrad's style because she does the "simple" thing so well. Her style is delicate, easy, and comfortable.

MAGAZINES. All the good ones, like *Seventeen*, *Teen Vogue*, and *InStyle*.

BLOGS. I'll go on style blogs and look at what people are posting for inspiration. I don't have a favorite blogger; instead, I usually go on Tumblr and do a search for things like "casual style" or "date outfits"—this way, I get inspiration from every kind of style under the sun!

STREET STYLE. To get ideas from anywhere in the world, I'll Google a city plus "street style." I'll search "L.A. Street Style," "Sydney Street Style," or "London Street Style." I love to draw style tips from raw photos of people just living their lives; they aren't in professional hair and makeup, but just out and about, on their way to school, work, or to meet up with friends . . . and that is as real as it gets.

Trying to Be "The Perfect Girl"

Before I embraced my own style, I liked being "The Perfect Girl." And my desperation to keep up with what pop culture deemed "hot" extended far beyond the "it" clothing item of the moment. I was listening to all the right songs and making sure to watch every trending show so I could keep up with the collective opinion I mistook for my own.

Then one day, I was being interviewed for a magazine story when the journalist asked me about my top favorite songs and styles. And while I was trying to answer, I suddenly realized: *I don't even know what I like anymore.* I was so worried about fitting in that I wasn't forming my own opinions at all. Instead, I was listening to the Top 20 songs, wearing the hot style trends, and claiming those as my favorites—when in reality, they *weren't*.

I had to really stop and think about what I loved. I had asked myself some of those questions before, here and there, but being challenged to come up with a truly personal list was the most fun I'd had in years.

Over time, I started doing, wearing, and listening to more and more things that weren't as trendy or popular. I wore what I felt the most comfortable in, and listened to what made me happy. If I felt like playing a Disney movie soundtrack, I would. If I wanted to wear sweats instead of jeans, I would. I started just *living*. And instantly, I felt better about my day-to-day. Keeping up with the Joneses is just so exhausting. There is seriously *no such thing* as being perfect. All you can do is listen to yourself and honor what you love—regardless of whether it's been featured in *Vogue*. Once you find the strength to be yourself, the rest will fall into place.

My Style Now

Whether you're two years old or twenty-two years old, getting dressed can be stressful (for different reasons, obviously). Sometimes, if I'm going to an event (it doesn't matter if it's at a casual restaurant or crazy red carpet), I'll obsess about what I think everyone else will be wearing. One of my biggest pet peeves is being either overdressed or underdressed. During the past few years, though, I've learned that the most important thing isn't how I look compared to everyone else, but how I feel.

That's why I keep my overall style very simple. I usually start an outfit with the basics, and then choose how I want to dress it up. Whether I want to look girly, or edgy, or sophisticated, every look begins with some classic staples—like my work button-up and blazer, or a pair of jeans—and then I build from there.

How I . . . Style My Jeans

I wear jeans more than anything else. And just so you know, when it comes to my jeans, I consider skinny jeans just . . . jeans. I don't own any boot cut or flares. I have a few different pairs, mostly from Rag & Bone or Nordstrom. But every pair is skinny, and I tend to style them in one of three ways.

COOL CASUAL

I've been doing this look a lot recently for a project where we work long hours and everyone is really laid back and hip, so I want to be comfortable and look current, too. The keys to this style are:

Roll the jeans: I might pull on my dark jeans with rips in the knees, and then cuff them twice.

Wear a printed T: I'll pair my jeans with a printed band T-shirt and, if it's chilly outside, top it with my leather jacket.

Add sneakers: My black Nikes complete this look.

DRESSY CASUAL

I love balancing girly pieces with something edgy—when combined, they make for a slightly dressier look. The keys to this style are:

High-waisted jeans: They're a bit more structured and work with shorter tops.

A feminine blouse: I have a silky black tank top with black lace trim that I recently paired with an oversized white blazer, with the sleeves rolled up.

Add heels: I'll add a chunky sandal or a thick-heeled boot that increases height. Then, for an edgy touch, maybe a black velvet choker or some layered gold necklaces.

COMFY CASUAL

If it's a chilly fall or winter day and I don't need to dress up, I'll usually default to this outfit. The keys to this style are:

Stretchy skinny jeans: I always choose a pair that has some give and stretch, since I'll be lounging around.

Wear an oversized cardigan: I have a super-thick, crazy comfortable big cardigan that's gray with a red tribal pattern on it. Because I pair it with the jeans, it doesn't look like I'm going out in my pajamas . . . but I feel like I'm living inside a marshmallow.

Add boots: I wear this with knee-high boots. Sometimes, I pull on a pair of fuzzy socks underneath them that you can't see, so I'm even cozier than people know.

Behind the Scenes: Creating My Fashion Line

When I was little, I always wondered what it would be like to design my own clothes. And as I grew up, I continued to think about it—but always as a "someday." And then, a couple of years ago, I was offered an opportunity by Aéropostale to literally make my dream come true.

It started when the brand invited me to breakfast with some of their executives. I didn't think anything was going to happen after that meeting, but they asked me to do a "meet and greet" in their Times Square store that July. I mentioned the meet and greet in a video, so a lot of my viewers came out—in fact, so many people came I was astonished! I seriously didn't expect a crowd that big. (Thank you if one of them was you!) This being one of my first major meet and greets, it was such an incredible gift to be able to see my viewers in person, beyond just reading their comments. I was so fired up about it, I stayed for six or seven hours, just hugging everyone—I didn't want to leave!

Then, they asked me to pick my favorite eight pieces from their fall collection, which they put on their website as "Bethany's Picks" that same summer. Those sold out, which was such a surreal moment. I love knowing that so many people trust my opinions—it's such an honor, and still so unbelievable!

I was having so much fun working with fashion, I considered going to fashion school so I could create my own clothing line. My dream was to attend FIDM (the Fashion Institute of Design & Merchandising in Los Angeles), but I could never find the time to apply, let alone attend, because I was so consumed by all of my YouTube work. So I began writing that "make a clothing line" goal down in my notebook, over and over again, because I was determined to make that dream come true. Well, the next thing I knew, I got another call from Aéropostale and they asked if I wanted to do a clothing line with them. I was *so* stoked! They must have been reading my mind.

I was lying in bed when I answered the phone, and I didn't move a muscle the whole time they were talking. I just lay there, almost speechless, not even processing what was happening. This was the opportunity of a lifetime—something I'd dreamed of as a little girl—and now it was about to come true. I could cross off "make a clothing line" in my dream journals, because it wasn't a dream anymore. It was reality. *My* reality. Somehow, the work that had been keeping me from attending fashion school in the first place—my passion for making videos on YouTube—had become

the very path that led straight to my goal! I couldn't believe it.

It was late summer when the Aéro team called, and they wanted to do a holiday collection.

"Okay," I said, "so we have a little over a year . . ." Clearly they didn't mean the holidays that were just a few months away, right?

"No," they said, "we want to launch it *this* year."

I was stunned; I didn't think you could put out a line that fast! I was also worried. The timeline meant I would really have to hustle, and couldn't overthink the process or second-guess myself about the designs; I just had to trust my gut. But I was up for the challenge, and I dove in. I've since learned that's when I produce the best: when I work fast and go with how I feel. I loved everything in that first collection.

I'll tell you this, though: Designing a line is *hard* work, and it really challenged me. When I was younger, the idea of being a fashion designer just seemed fun—raise the hem of this skirt here, make this T-shirt a long-sleeved shirt there, add buttons and details and patterns everywhere. But actually doing it? There is a lot more to think about than I had realized. Yes, I'd been given a blank canvas with which I could do whatever I wanted. The options were limitless, and that was the problem: It's hard to concretely conceptualize a piece of clothing when you have so many choices ahead of you—and here I was, designing a whole line! There are so many

details that go into each item of clothing. If I wanted to make a blouse, I had to decide: What kind of fabric should it be? What color? What pattern? What collar should it have? And so on. My biggest issue, in fact, was being indecisive. Often, each decision came down to two options: "Do you want to go with this logo or that logo?" or "Which button do you want?" And I remember feeling like I needed a few days to think about that—if you're wearing one of my Aéro pieces right now, trust me: it took me days to pick those buttons!

My favorite part of the process was playing with ideas. I would go on Pinterest and search through Google and Tumblr to help spur my creativity, and then we'd put together these huge inspiration boards. I was completely immersed in the creative side of it. But the best part of doing the line overall was the samples: After I designed something, they would send me a sample of it in the mail. I had picked the cut and the pattern and the color—not to mention the millions of other details that went into it—and now, there I was in the mirror, *wearing it on my body*.

When you're putting on a piece of clothing, you don't usually think about those little details, but now I do. And I'm grateful that I can now look at fashion through that very specific lens. The whole experience gave me a new appreciation for designers, and now I love being even more creative with my style based on what I learned.

When I Spend vs. When I Save

My wardrobe is a pretty even balance between quality staple items I've invested in and cheaper trendy pieces. When deciding whether to save or splurge, I'll ask myself if I'll wear or use that particular item for years to come. If I'm looking to buy a classic staple, like a leather jacket or a pair of skinny jeans, I'm more likely to invest.

If you're able to, I think you should save up and spend a bit more on certain items in your closet. Think of it in fashion-math terms: Instead of buying three shirts of poor quality that will fall apart or start fraying quickly, you can invest in one item you'll have for years. So when you compare the prices of those purchases over time, you'll actually spend *less* money buying a better-made item. And if I am splurging on a classic item like a carryall or a pair of shoes, I'll choose a neutral color, such as black, white, or camel, that I'll love and use as much years down the line. (I won't splurge on a crazy print or a bold color like hot pink, because I know I won't carry or wear it as much.)

One of my biggest splurges was a black Céline bag I travel with that I chose to spend money on. It's very structured, my laptop fits in it nicely, and I never have to worry about it falling apart the way a super-cheap version of it would, what with all the physical demands I put on the bag. Yes, I had to save for that purchase, but I felt empowered that I had worked hard enough to buy it for myself.

RANDOM ME FACT: JEWELRY AND I DON'T GET ALONG

I love delicate jewelry, but I don't wear it very often—because I cannot keep jewelry on me to save my life! I lose it constantly. Seriously, the reason I'm very minimal with accessories and don't buy expensive jewelry is that I just can't keep them on my body. I actually have so many holes in my ears and no earrings right now because the earrings fell out. I don't know how that happened . . . they just did. I have no clue where my jewelry goes, it just . . . I don't know, disappears into thin air or is absorbed into the earth. There's probably a graveyard for all the bobby pins and jewelry I've lost over the years—and I'd do anything to visit it!

DIY: Make Your Own Crystal Jewelry

I lose my jewelry so often that I literally wish I could glue it onto my body. But since I can't do that (well, at least it would look super-weird if I did), I started to DIY my own jewelry out of inexpensive wire so I wouldn't care as much if I lost it. This is one of my favorite pieces.

WHAT YOU'LL NEED

A plain ring band, a crystal, wire from the craft store, and wire cutters. If you don't have a ring band, you can also create the band out of wire, wrapping it around your finger to form a ring shape.

HOW TO MAKE IT

Step 1: Wrap your crystal with a small piece of wire so that it is completely enclosed and can't fall out. Your piece of wire should be long enough to wrap the crystal and your ring finger, so give yourself a lot to work with—maybe about twelve inches. With one end of the wire at the bottom of the crystal, pull the remaining length of wire up along one side. Twist the wire around the crystal twice, then back down to the bottom of the crystal—so it is enclosed on four sides—for the next step.

Step 2: Wrap the remaining wire around the top of your ring band two or three times. If you don't have a ring band, wrap the wire around your finger to form a ring shape.

Step 3: Tuck the wire ends beneath your crystal. Wear happily!

I'm Obsessed with . . . Online Shopping

I do most of my shopping online. I love that I can open ten tabs of my favorite stores so I can see them side by side, which helps me compare small details on each item, as well as build outfits between them.

These days, my favorite sites belong to Australian clothing brands. That's because when I went to the malls in Australia, I realized how effortlessly stylish and chic Australian women are. They really master the "I look like I'm not trying" laid-back look. My favorite Aussie online shops are:

- Sabo Skirt
- Glue Store
- Princess Polly
- Revolve

MY 2 BEST STYLE TRICKS

I'M ALL ABOUT THAT WAIST. One night, I went out in a long-sleeved, zip-up, black peplum top with black jeans, and it looked *so* good—but even better, I ate a big dinner that night and the peplum totally disguised my food baby! So I love dresses or tops that cinch in the waistline and then flare out a little. It's such a flattering, girly shape that complements every woman's body.

I'M ALWAYS ELONGATING. Since I'm just five-foot-three, I'm usually thinking about ways to make myself look a little taller—and though heels are a tiny girl's best friend, perfectly tailored pants come in at a close second! I prefer pants that go all the way down past my ankle to make my legs appear longer. Cropped pants and wide, flowy pants can make me look a little more compact and boxy.

My Dressing-Room Secrets

As I mentioned, I love online shopping. But if I am on a mission and need something specific, I will go out alone to shop in stores. I shop with friends when I'm browsing and hanging out, but if I need a particular item fast, then I need to be by myself (seriously, I gotta focus!). These are my techniques that help me make the most of my shopping day.

1. *I wear easy-to-pull-off clothes so I can try things on easily.* Over the years, I've bought tons of clothes without trying them on in the store because I was wearing a really complicated outfit—and couldn't bear to take it off in the dressing room. Half the time, when I got it home, the item wouldn't fit right and I'd have to return it anyway. So as annoying as it is sometimes, you absolutely have to try things on to know if they will work for you; you can't judge something by how it looks on a mannequin or hanger. I like to wear a simple, stretchy dress and a pair of flats, or even a T-shirt and jeans when I shop—as long as a wiggle situation isn't happening because my jeans are too tight.

2. *When I like something, I ask myself, "Do I have something in my closet like this already?"* If you have a certain style, you tend to be attracted to the same thing over and over, and before you know it, you have five of the same top! (Well, at least I know I do.) So right before I try something on, I think, "It's really cute, so . . . do I already have something like it?"

3. *I try on a whole outfit.* If I find a skirt that I think will look good with a white tank top and heels, I'll grab any white tank top and pair of heels in the store to try on with it, just to see what it looks like. I won't end up buying the tank top or the shoes, but it's nice to actually see what the skirt looks like when paired with a full outfit.

4. *I take selfies from all angles—even the back.* I don't know what it is, but there's something about looking at a photo of you in an outfit that gives you a different perspective on how it fits. So whenever I'm taking forever in the dressing room, it's probably because I'm snapping tons of mirror pics and selfies from literally every angle. (Okay, maybe not that one angle looking up at my outfit from below—*so* not flattering.)

5. *I'll sometimes send the photo to a friend.* If you have a friend you trust to ask for advice, definitely get his or her opinion if you're unsure about the piece you're trying on.

6. *I picture myself wearing it in a social setting.* A lot of times, we can like the *idea* of something, but we can't figure out where we'd actually wear it. So I'll picture myself in different scenarios: I'll imagine myself wearing the outfit at a social event, a birthday party, or a dinner, and see if it feels right. Sometimes I'll realize that the outfit doesn't vibe with the event I'll want to wear it to, and that saves me a lot of time and money.

7. *I do a "comfy" check.* The most important thing I test is whether or not I'm going to be comfortable moving around in something. So if I'm trying on an outfit for an event, I'll pose and look at it from the side, I'll sit down, I'll make big hand gestures as if I'm talking to someone, and I'll even do a little dancing. I want to make sure the outfit allows me to do everything I want to do. Because if I don't feel comfortable doing all those things in the dressing room, then I know I'll feel self-conscious about them in public!

Closet Inspo: What I Love About My Closet

Getting dressed in the morning is stressful enough—but if my closet is a mess, it stresses me out even more! I do my best to keep a clean, organized space, so I can clearly see what I have and start my day off right.

- My dresser is for super-casual T-shirts, shorts, workout wear, yoga pants, sweaters, sports bras, and pajamas. There are probably more yoga pants than anything—I think I have a dozen of each style of Lululemon yoga pants! (Okay, I'm exaggerating a little. But I definitely have more pairs than one human needs!)

- My hangers are for my jeans, skirts, dresses, and scarves. I like having an instant visual of what I have, because when clothes are folded in dressers, I have to tear the drawer apart to see everything. I like to avoid making a huge mess before my day has really begun, so for the most part, my day-to-day wear is all hanging.

- My shelves are for my belts and hats, even though I don't have a lot of either. I have two or three belts—I have a thick black belt I wear with jeans, a button-up, and heels; and a brown belt that's a little thinner. Any more and I would be overwhelmed. Likewise, I only have three or four hats; I just don't wear hats very much.

- My shoes are just lined up on the floor. I'd love to say I have them perfectly organized in pretty, labeled boxes, but I don't. I do find that keeping them all out and clearly visible helps me match them with my outfits.

- I try to get rid of clothes I don't wear often. If I haven't worn a certain item of clothing in a month or two and have no desire to wear it anytime soon, then it's just taking up space. I give away most of those items, either to a charity, or to family and friends.

When I Wear the "Wrong" Thing

It's happened to me before: I've walked into a room and realized I clearly missed the memo and was either totally overdressed or underdressed. But what I've learned is that you have two options in those situations: You can isolate yourself or you can just own it.

If I give into the emotion of feeling uncomfortable, I don't enjoy the actual event I'm attending. But if I make a beeline for people I know, I can have a good conversation that distracts me from my self-consciousness.

And once I begin to enjoy myself, I usually realize that people don't care what I'm wearing, because they're either too busy enjoying themselves, or they're wrapped up in thinking about what *they're* wearing!

So now, if I'm dressed differently than everyone else, I choose to rock my look instead of let it get me down. I want people to remember *me*—and anyone who's going to judge me based on my outfit isn't worth my time, anyway.

MY "DANCE IT OUT" STYLE TEST

One time I wore a short dress to a day full of events, but I didn't realize *how* short it was until I wore it in public. Have you ever had one of those dresses where every time you move, it hikes up? Well, it was one of those. I was adjusting it constantly while we were walking around, and then I'd adjust it again after I sat down. At one point, we had to take some escalators, and all I could think was "Oh, awesome, everyone behind me can see up my dress." I was on edge all day.

I now have a method for testing if an outfit will work for me: When I'm getting ready, I dance in it—even if I am going to a business meeting. While I'm dancing, I tell myself, "No matter what I do today, I probably won't be moving more than I am *right now*." If the outfit passes the dance test, I know I'll be good—no matter what craziness a day throws my way.

6

Beauty

{ Beauty to me isn't just about makeup anymore.
Beauty really begins with what we put into our bodies. }

Rethinking Beauty (aka Go Away Acne!)

I used to have a lot of acne. When I was thirteen, I didn't have an issue with bad skin, but at fourteen and fifteen, something happened. (Well, I know what happened—I was going through puberty!) Suddenly I had acne on my forehead and on my chin, and then it started making its way to all of the areas in between. Eventually, I had zits all over my face, all the time.

This happened to be about the time when I was first getting into makeup, and the acne was distracting from my look—I felt that my awesome eye shadow didn't look as good because I had blemishes on my cheeks that were stealing the spotlight. There are even a

few of my YouTube makeup tutorials where you can clearly see my acne. No matter what I did, it seemed like it would always be there, front and center.

Still, I tried *everything* to get rid of it; I used every product in the book. I tried a pink serum that went on as a liquid but dried and stung. And I tried a spot treatment that smelled really gross and just didn't feel like it belonged on my face. I remember thinking that the crazy products I was trying couldn't be good for my skin. And they weren't; I was using so many chemicals and switching them out so frequently that it was actually doing more harm than good.

Over time, my acne started to go away on its own. Maybe it was because I was growing up, or maybe it was because I wasn't obsessing about it and stopped using strong chemicals (it was probably a combination of both), but it slowly disappeared.

Now I'm very minimal with how I take care of my skin. I have very sensitive and oily skin, so I tend to use just a few cleansing products—like foam washes and masks— with gentle ingredients that will be easy on my skin. But most important, I care about what I put into my body, so my skin glows healthfully from the inside out.

My beauty style is simple: It starts with a good complexion. Yes, blemishes still pop up (oh, do they!), and that's okay. When you know you're doing your best for your skin, you can accept the blemishes and enjoy makeup more, because it becomes less about the necessity and all about the art and the fun.

BEAUTY FROM THE INSIDE OUT

Beauty to me isn't just about makeup anymore. Beauty really begins with what we put into our bodies. By eating right, I end up with radiant skin, fewer blemishes, and an overall happy glow that is reflected on my face. Here are the ways I treat my body better through what I eat and drink so that my skin looks beautiful, every day:

1. I cut out soda and sugary drinks. Back when I was younger, I never liked water, so I drank a lot of soda and sugary beverages instead. But I rarely drink soda now, and that switch has hugely benefited my skin.

2. I eat foods with a lot of water in them. I eat salads full of spinach, kale, and cucumbers. It's a way to get extra water through your meal. The more you hydrate, the more your skin glows from the inside out.

3. I eat tons of avocados. The monounsaturated fats in them basically moisturize your skin from the inside, to keep it soft, plump, and healthy.

Bethany's Beauty-Full Avocado Toast

I eat avocado a *lot*. Sometimes for a snack I'll cut an avocado in half and eat it plain with lime juice. Or, I'll make my favorite avocado toast for a mid-morning boost!

INGREDIENTS

2 pieces of Ezekiel bread
1 avocado
1 lime, juiced
salt and pepper, to taste
red chili flakes

TO MAKE THE TOAST

Step 1: Toast the bread.

Step 2: Cut the avocado in half, remove the pit with a spoon, and scoop the avocado into a bowl. Gently mash the avocado, adding the lime juice and mixing together.

Step 3: Spread the avocado and lime on the toast.

Step 4: Top with salt, pepper, and a sprinkle of red chili flakes.

My Skincare Routine

When I was growing up, my skincare routine was as easy as it gets. My mom used to tell me, "Keep it simple and wash your face with water." So that's literally all I did as a kid. Then I went through my awful acne phase where I was constantly testing very harsh products on my face. Now the way I take care of my skin is simple once again: I don't touch my skin a lot, I have cut out sugary foods and drinks from my diet, I never sleep in my makeup, and I have a skincare routine that's saved my face. I do this routine morning and night.

AT NIGHT

Step 1: I gently remove all of my face makeup. First, to remove my eye makeup, I'll put some liquid remover (I currently like Neutrogena's eye makeup remover) on some cotton pads and use them to gently rub off my eyeliner, eye shadow, and mascara. Then, I'll use the Josie Maran Bear Naked Wipes to remove my face makeup. (In a pinch, if I'm out of wipes, I'll also just run a fresh cotton pad or two soaked with the eye makeup remover over my face to get that clean, too—hey, if it works, it works!)

Step 2: I use sheet masks a couple of times a week and love the individually packaged face masks by Sephora. I either use the Pearl (which brightens skin) or the Lotus (super-hydrating) mask, depending what my skin needs. They're white paper sheet masks with all the cutouts for your eyes, nose, and mouth, and they're covered in serum. I just lay one of them on my face . . . and look terrifying! Then I lie down on my bed for about thirty minutes, peel off the mask, and rub the remaining serum into my face. It's like a little mini spa night. Sometimes the mask feels so good, I'll forget it's on my face. I haven't yet answered the door when I've forgotten I'm wearing one, but knowing me, that will probably happen at some point and I'll scare the Postmates delivery person away!

Step 3: I'll wash my face. I use Lancôme Énergie de Vie Foam Cleanser most nights; then, about twice a week, I'll use Tatcha Classic Rice Enzyme Powder for a deeper clean. It's a powder cleanser that, when mixed with water, turns into an exfoliating foam that washes away dirt and oil.

Step 4: I will use the Clarisonic Brush two to three times a month on my face and neck for one minute, until my face is squeaky clean.

Step 5: I'll put on moisturizer. I use this Korean one called Su:m37 Water-full Rebalancing Gel Lotion. It's the perfect combination of deeply nourishing and yet light-weight, and it absorbs into my skin almost immediately.

IN THE MORNING

Step 1: I'll remove any excess makeup. If there's a little bit of eyeliner left from the day before, I'll take it off with a Q-tip and makeup remover.

Step 2: I'll clean my face with warm water on a towel to open and cleanse my pores. Then, I'll splash cold water on it to close my pores right back up.

Step 3: I'll re-moisturize, just enough to prep my skin for makeup.

How I . . . Do My Foundation

I get my makeup done a lot for events, and I've learned so much from the makeup artists I've worked with over the years. My two favorite makeup artists are Kip Zachary, who I've worked with for over two years, and Lauren Anderson. When they're doing my makeup, I can't help but observe their techniques and tips, so I've naturally picked up a few pointers (thanks, guys!). One of the tricks that has worked its way into my everyday routine is how I apply my foundation, which consists of a few steps—and includes one really cool pro tip.

When you're applying your makeup, a flawless base can change your look completely—and allow you to have fun with the rest!

Step 1: First, I apply moisturizer all over my face, and let it sink in for a few minutes. A dry face isn't a good start for all the blending you'll be doing. I don't use a foundation primer, because my moisturizer smooths out my skin enough, so I don't need that extra step.

Step 2: I'll apply liquid foundation—my favorite now is Make Up For Ever Ultra HD. (I tend to use foundations that give a dewy effect. If you aren't sure which foundations would work best with your skin, you can always check in with a makeup artist at your local department store or Sephora!) I put one pump of liquid foundation on the back of my hand, and pick it up with an Airbrush foundation brush from Sephora that's light and fluffy rather than dense. Then, to apply it all over my face, I begin with circular strokes, starting from my T-zone and working my way outward. Using the same brush, I stipple the foundation all over my face, then finish with circular motions again to blend the foundation in completely. It's a process, but it works to smooth out the foundation to a flawless finish.

Step 3: I use a beautyblender sponge (which is a little foam-like egg) and just pat and dab it all over my face to smooth what I've already applied.

***A little tip:** You have to wet the beautyblender and wring it out before you use it, which I never knew! I used one for a while and thought it didn't really work for me, but realized that when you wet it, it gets bigger and softer and blends the foundation more naturally. I store mine on a little stand that sits on my counter so the blender can dry completely (and hygienically!) between uses.

Step 4: In three areas, I apply a concealer two shades lighter than my actual skin color, to highlight my face: under my eyes, on the bridge of my nose, and on my chin. I blend the concealer in with the same beautyblender, and then I move on to my favorite pro tip.

Step 5: The Pro-Tip: I love to "bake" my skin—and not in the sun! After I apply my foundation and concealer, I dab a layer of loose powder over the concealer and along my jawline. To apply, sprinkle some loose powder on your hand, pick it up with a dry wedge sponge, and dab it on desired areas. I let it sit (aka bake) for five to ten minutes.

Step 6: While the powder is "baking," I dust on bronzer in three areas: on my cheekbones, temples, and neck.

Step 7: Once the powder is done baking for those five to ten minutes, I buff it away with a buffer brush. That whole process "bakes" the powder on so that your makeup stays in place all day!

Step 8: I spray M.A.C's Fix+ finishing mist all over my face to keep my face looking fresh. Sometimes when you put a powder on your face, it looks really dull and, well, powdery; when I add the spray, it combats the overly dry look and keeps my makeup in place.

My Beauty Style

I tend to apply my makeup as natural-looking as possible, because I want people to notice me for *me* instead of what's on my face (plus, I don't want my makeup to distract from my outfit).

In fact, I often purposely plan my makeup to complement my outfit. So if I'm wearing a busy pattern or a lot of colors, I'll wear very muted, nude, or matte tones of eye shadow, and a natural lip. It's important to have a balance between your makeup, clothing, and hair so that nothing overpowers or competes with anything else.

My Daily Brow Makeup

Step 1: I brush through my brows before I apply brow makeup, to set the shape. (I just get big packages of cheap brow brushes, because I lose them the same way I lose hair ties and jewelry!)

Step 2: I'll highlight my brows, using a brow pencil or brow powder, to create a sharp line across the top and the bottom of each brow. I'll either use my Anastasia liner, or brow powder with an angled brush.

Step 3: I'll fill in the inside of the brow with brow powder—but I'll only use a tiny bit and apply the powder in the direction the hair is going.

*A little tip: I try not to outline or fill the brows in too much; I did that once and it looked like I painted them on! You should be enhancing the natural shape and fullness of the brow, not creating a new one altogether.

JUST BROWS-ING

I got my first pair of tweezers when I was eleven. But I didn't understand the idea that they were used to shape your eyebrows; I thought they were meant for removing a bunch of hair overall. So I went into my room alone, thinking, "Gross! So much hair on my eyebrows!" and I just plucked away. I wasn't going for an arch or a shape. My only goal was "Less hair!"

Well . . . I plucked out so much hair, my mom was mad at me! And my eyebrows were never the same after that; I think it's why my eyebrows are so uneven to this day.

The left one sits a little higher. People love to remind me of that—in my video comments! Really, my left brow only gets noticeably higher when I'm making dramatic expressions. So if you've noticed it yourself (or start to), think of it this way: It just means I'm passionate! I've also accepted that's how mine are, so I do my best to just keep them neat and touch them up when I'm doing my makeup.

Now, tending to my brows is a big thing for me. I consider them to be one of the focal points of my face. Even if I don't wear a lot of makeup one day, I will still focus on my brows, so I try to take good care of mine.

I get them waxed about every month and a half. I always tell the person doing my brows to keep them very full, because the first time I got my brows done, the waxer made them too thin. Another time I got them done, the lady made my higher brow even more dramatic, and that lasted awhile. So you have to be clear about what shape you want, because if they mess up, it takes a long time for that hair to grow back.

My 3 Favorite Eye Looks

There are three basic ways I do my eye makeup. The technique for each one is more about the method than the color I use. For instance, I use a lot of brown tones on my eyes, but you could also use blues or silvers or even brighter colors with the same exact technique. Note: I get eyelash extensions professionally done, so I don't use mascara on my top lashes. Here are the steps I use to achieve each look.

EYE LOOK #1: NATURAL EYE

This is a very simple, light, and airy look.

Step 1: I start with an eye shadow primer, such as the one made by Urban Decay. I like to apply a dollop of product to the back of my hand, and then blend it into my lids and up to my brow bone with my ring finger. (A lot of the new tubes are equipped with a wand, but I like mine in the squeezy tube.) Eye shadow primer is the key to keeping the eyelids from getting oily throughout the day. It also extends the wear of a shadow and keeps it from collecting in the crease of the lid. If I run out of primer, I just use my concealer, because I find it works just as well.

Step 2: I apply bronzer to the crease of my lid, by using a big fluffy eye shadow brush to blend, blend, blend. Don't worry about being too precise here; it's just a wash of color. And . . . that's it. This look is light and airy, but still polished!

EYE LOOK #2: SMOKY EYE

This look is an ombré for the eyes: It's darkest closest to your lashes, a medium tone in your crease, and lightest closest to the brow bone. Get ready for your eyes to pop!

Step 1: I apply an eye shadow primer.

Step 2: I sweep a medium, neutral color eye shadow all over my lid and crease. I like to use

a flat brush to pat color onto my eyelid. Then, I switch to a fluffy brush to blend the same color into my crease, starting at the corners, and blending from the outer corner in. I usually use a matte brown or medium matte brown, nothing super-dark. I feel like natural tones work for everyone on a day-to-day basis, such as the colors you'd find in the Naked palette by Urban Decay.

Step 3: I apply a cream-colored shadow to my brow bone, then apply that same shadow to the inner corner of each eye to brighten the overall look. I might add a light dash of a bronzer on my browbone, too.

Step 4: I apply a dark shadow on the upper lash line in place of liquid liner, smudging it with a tiny, tapered eye shadow brush. (With my skin tone, a chocolate-hued matte brown works best.) Then, I apply the same hue along my lower lash line, and smudge it with the tapered brush. It gives my whole eye an awesome smoky effect.

Step 5: I'll add a black pencil liner along my waterline at the base of my eye—like the one from Honest Beauty﹣and a swipe of mascara on my bottom lashes.

EYE LOOK #3: DRAMATIC EYE

This will have a softly "cut crease," which is almost like a reverse ombré look.

Step 1: I start by applying eye shadow primer.

Step 2: I will apply a light, cream-colored or champagne-colored shadow all over my entire lid and up to my brow bone; I also apply it to the inner corner of each eye.

Step 3: I blend a slightly darker shadow into the crease.

Step 4: Then—and this is the fun part—I'll apply a slightly darker colored shadow to the outer corner of the crease of my lid. I use an angled brush to apply color to the outer corner areas of my eyes, then I blend the color into the crease as well.

Step 5: I run a dark liquid liner across my lash line, and wing it out a little bit. When I was first learning how to wing my liner, I used

Scotch tape to help me define a sharp edge, but I haven't been using tape lately. It's important that the line has a natural angle, almost as if it's an extension of your outer eyelashes. One foolproof way for figuring out where the tip should end? I sometimes start my wing where I want it to end, then I draw the line *backwards*, in toward my eyelid. Ultimately, I find that getting a good wing point is just practice. It's all about bravery, boldness, and just going for it!

⁺A little tip: You can also use a gel liner; dip an angled eye brush into a gel pot and apply along your lash line. Liquid liner is faster for me, but my chances of messing it up are higher; gel gives me more control.

Saving Face

I'm Portuguese, so I never burn, but I tan really easily. When I was a little kid playing outside with my sister all the time, I would get so dark. But what's funny is that my sister never tans, so she would stay really light, and people used to think we weren't related!

Even though I don't burn, I always wear sunscreen. I like the spray-on ones for convenience, and I spray them on places I know aren't covered by clothes, like my arms and legs. And if I want to look tan, I get a spray tan.

I got my first spray tan three years ago. I was like, "I'm scared I'm going to be orange!" But it was great. Spray tans are a really good way to get a tan quickly, especially in the summer, when I want to wear brighter colors. Yet instead of sitting outside in the sun for hours, you're evenly tan in fifteen minutes.

If you're going to get a spray tan for a special event, though, trust me: Do it the day before so it doesn't end up rubbing off on your outfit and ruining your clothes. The one time I got a spray tan on the day of the event, I wore a white dress, and by the time I got home, the entire inside of the dress was brown! I never made that mistake again.

I also learned the hard way that you should let the tan develop for a few hours, and then rinse it off in the shower. How do I know this? Because one time I went straight to bed after my spray tan session, then woke up to see that my tan legs had two white handprints on my thighs! I was so confused until I saw my palms: They were dark brown. True story. Classic Bethany. I couldn't wear a skirt or shorts for days! So take it from me on the spray tan tricks.

If you do it right, you get some nice, even color. And you'll also save your skin from short-term and long-term damage, making it much safer for your overall health—which is really the best part of all.

Mastering the Matte Lip

I love a good matte lip. I tend to save bold matte looks for the fall and winter (burgundy or dark browns are my go-tos), but I'll rock a lighter matte liquid lipstick in a dusty-rose shade all year long. Here's my process.

Step 1: Sometimes I will condition my lips first, because I find the liner goes on a lot smoother if I do. (I've had times where I've tried to apply a lip pencil, and it breaks because my lips are too dry!) The conditioner I use now is an olive oil lip balm that I got in Greece, similar to the size of a ChapStick. It's unscented, very natural, and not too creamy—it's just hydrating enough to soften my lips.

Step 2: I line my lips with a good pencil liner, like the ones I get from M.A.C, in the same shade as the lipstick. I tend to follow the natural line of my lips (though I will occasionally overline just a little bit). Then I'll fill in the rest of my lips with the liner to create an even base.

Step 3: I'll apply a liquid matte lipstick within my natural lip line—Kat Von D makes a really great liquid lipstick. And . . . that's it. When I do my lips this way, I can drink and eat anything I want without risking losing my color!

My 3 Basic Makeup Routines

My makeup routine changes depending on where I'm going and how much time I have. Basically, I have three versions of my beauty routine, which I've paired here with my three favorite eye looks from pages 116–117.

ROUTINE #1: SUPER QUICK

It takes about five minutes, so I use this one if I'm running late or if I'm on the go. I've done this one in a car before!

Step 1: Rub in a tinted moisturizer.

Step 2: Add a little bit of loose powder under my eyes.

Step 3: Do my brows, outlining them and filling them in with a brow pencil or shadow. (See "My Daily Brow Makeup" tutorial on page 114.)

Step 4: I'll do the "natural eye" look (p. 116) then apply mascara to my bottom lashes.

Step 5: Add a bronzer blush to my cheekbones.

Step 6: Finish with a natural-color gloss on my lips for a little shine, like M.A.C Plushgloss in Ample Pink.

ROUTINE #2: MEDIUM-ISH

This one takes twenty to thirty minutes. I use it most often, on a daily basis. This is my look for a casual day or if I don't have much to do.

Step 1: Put on liquid foundation. I pump a dab of foundation onto the back of my hand, then blend it onto my face using an Airbrush foundation brush from Sephora.

Step 2: Blend a little bit of concealer under my eyes.

Step 3: Do my brows the same way I would in the quick version, outlining them and filling them in with a brow pencil or shadow.

Step 4: Apply eye shadow primer.

Step 5: Instead of full-on eye shadow, I'll dust bronzer on my eyelids with my eye shadow brush to give my face a sun-kissed look. You don't have to be precise, but a small swipe gives you a little color.

RANDOM ME FACT:
I'M NOT A PINK BLUSH PERSON

I prefer using blush in bronze-like tones such as peaches and neutrals, and I always try to focus the blush on the upper part of my cheekbone. I will rarely go for a red or pink blush, and I won't put it on the apples of my cheeks, because I always end up looking like a doll—or like a seven-year-old experimenting with makeup for the first time!

Step 6: I'll do something like the "smoky eye" look (p. 116), then apply mascara to my bottom lashes.

Step 7: Add bronze-colored blush to my cheekbones, jawline, nose, and my neck. I like NARS and M.A.C for their dusty plum colors (I've played with a few of the different shades in those tones), and I love the Cheek to Chic blush from Charlotte Tilbury in a peach tone (my current fave is the Ecstasy palate, with a slightly shimmery highlight color in the center of the pan).

Step 8: Apply powder to set everything. I don't "bake" my foundation in this case, as I don't have enough time.

Step 9: Spray my whole face and neck with finishing spray.

Step 10: For my lips, I apply a thin layer of Milk Makeup Lip Salve, then I tap on some raspberry color with Neutrogena Moisture Smooth Color Stick in Bright Berry. Then, I mix the two with a lip brush to create the perfect natural lip with a little pop.

ROUTINE #3: THE LONG HAUL

This one takes about 1.5 hours . . . but that includes time for singing and dancing!
Without the singing and dancing, it only takes about forty-five minutes. I use it if
I'm going somewhere very significant, like an event or party. Or on the days I just
feel like going all out with it, even if I'm only going to the dry cleaners.

Step 1: Apply liquid foundation.

Step 2: Blend some concealer under my eyes
to highlight the area a bit, which makes me
look more awake.

Step 3: "Bake" my concealer and powder,
which can take up to ten minutes. (See the
Pro-Tip on page 113.)

Step 4: Add bronzer to my cheekbones by my
temples.

Step 5: Do my brows.

Step 6: Spend extra time on my eyes with a
more complex "dramatic eye" look (p. 117),
then add mascara on the bottom lashes—I
still don't put any mascara on top.

Step 7: Contour with my bronzer. I'll add it
to my cheekbones, nose, jawline, and
neck.

Step 8: Dab a shimmer stick on my cheekbones
in a neutral shade. The stick itself almost resembles a fat crayon. I apply it to my cheekbones
with a small swiping movement, then dab over
it with a damp beautyblender (I'll wet it, then
squeeze out the excess water) to blend it out so
it looks more natural. This creates a really pretty
glow and brightens my face when my skin hits
the light. This is great for a night out.

Step 9: Dust a bronze-colored blush higher up
on my cheekbones in a neutral color.

Step 10: Do my lips to complete the look.
I will line my lips with a M.A.C lip pencil in
Oak, then apply M.A.C's Peachstock lipstick,
and finish it off with some Sweet Peach
Creamy Peach Oil lip gloss from Too Faced to
give my lips a luscious shine.

Step 11: Top it all with the Fix+ finishing
spray.

Getting
SOCIAL

How I find and build relationships through friends and dating

Other people's energy is so contagious. That's why I like to surround myself with great people who will help me grow. One of my top priorities in life is to create and nourish bonds with people who only better my life—because after all, if you have a solid support system around you for all of the ups and the downs life throws your way, nothing else matters. The stronger your group of friends is, and the more authentic your relationships are, the happier you will be.

7

Friends

{ *I work hard to surround myself with people who are motivated, positive, and passionate about life.* }

Feeling Out of Place

When I was six, I was in the movie theater seeing *Lilo & Stitch*. I remember watching one of the opening scenes where Lilo wants to play dolls with the other girls in the group, but they're mean to her and her beaten-up little stuffed animal, Scrump. The girls just walk away from Lilo and leave her standing there alone. And during that scene in the theater, little me just started bawling. That was the first time I remember being emotional and feeling genuinely sad. Even though I was a kid, I just felt that scene so deeply. I remember even trying to hide my face in the theater, because I was crying *so* hard. I guess I'm

sensitive to that feeling because I've felt left out like that before—and sometimes, I still feel that way.

Maybe I'll be at a party where everyone else already seems to know each other, so I feel like I'm intruding; or maybe a group is discussing things I'm not familiar with, like a show or book or movie that just came out. I used to do this thing where I'd attempt to engage in conversation while hiding the fact that I had no idea what I was talking about. ("Oh, I've heard of that band! Their one single is really, um, good . . .). But I've found the best thing to do is *own* the fact that I'm not in the loop instead of feeling self-conscious about it, and see it as an opportunity to learn something from someone else. Hey, so what if I get the name of a show wrong or confuse the author of a book or admit to liking a movie everyone thinks is the worst one ever? Maybe I can grow from it. Because the bottom line is, if I'm only participating in a conversation to impress other people, I'm disrespecting myself! So my main priorities now are learning about others and developing a connection. And I can't learn anything if I'm sitting in the corner; and I can't have a true connection with someone if I'm not letting my walls down.

MY GOING-OUT BAG

I've finally found my favorite bag for when I go out with friends, so I no longer have to stress about choosing one when I'm getting ready. My go-to right now is a black quilted Chanel bag that I invested in. I love it because it not only goes with everything I wear, but it also takes every outfit to the next level, so it's perfect to take to events. I have a Topshop cross-body bag that I love, too, that costs almost nothing and has all the same features. Here's what I look for in a going-out bag:

MEDIUM SIZE. I want a size that's big enough to fit my phone, wallet, and keys, along with a deodorant stick or some mini perfume if I know it will be a long night.

CROSS-BODY STYLE. It's important to me that my bag has a strap. When I'm out, I want to have my purse on me at all times, so I don't have to stress about keeping my eye on it. A cross-body is really nice, because then I can dance with it on, and I don't have to hold a clutch the whole time.

SMALL POCKETS. I like one with a lot of pockets, so if I want to stick a business card or a valet ticket in there, it won't get lost at the bottom of my bag.

What's in My Bag?

I always bring: My phone, wallet, keys, blotting sheets, a light pink plumping lip gloss, gum (usually Extra Polar Ice), a little comb to keep my hair in check, and a powder for a quick touch-up or two.

The weirdest thing I carry: One single earring, for a style emergency. Sometimes I'll wear a shirt that opens up too far, and if need be, I can clip it back together with a little stud earring. It has to be a strong earring, but it works. I started using the earring out of convenience when I needed something to clamp my shirt closed and plucked a shiny little stud right out of my ear. And since you can sometimes accidentally see a safety pin, the earring is my preferred choice, because it adds a pretty detail while doing the job. So now I tend to keep one little rhinestone crystal earring in the side pocket of my purse.

My must-have party item: My iPhone LuMee case. It lights up to provide all the radiant light you need to nail that middle-of-the-night selfie.

The Challenge of Meeting New People

The first time I went to a party alone, it was terrifying. It was an event in someone's house and I knew *no one.*

When I walked in, there were groups of people clustered together. I scanned the room to find someone standing alone, but I couldn't find one. So then I looked for groups I could fit myself into, but they all seemed too tight-knit for me to interrupt and say hello. So I did something I use now all the time: I made my way over to the drinks table for a water and kept my eyes open for someone who was wearing something I liked, whether it was a top, shoes or even a nail polish color. Soon, I saw a girl wearing an adorable dress, so I just said, "I love your dress. Where did you get it?" And we ended up having a conversation that led to me meeting some of her friends.

I've found that this is a really good way to start conversations—but only if I have an

HAVING A BAD TIME AT THE PARTY? MY 3 TRICKS

There have been times when I'm at a party, and I want to leave. But in cases where it was rude to go early or I just wasn't able to sneak out yet, I found that if I changed my mindset, I was able to start enjoying the night. I've done it so many times now that I have a few tricks to help shift my thinking when I need to.

1. I'll look at the situation from a larger perspective. Like, I will literally try to picture the situation from above. And as soon as I do that, I'll realize, "There are people here who are into cool things I can learn about" or "Maybe I can meet someone who needs a good laugh." Seeing things through a wider lens helps me stop being so wrapped up in my own emotions and start considering that there are other people in the room who might feel like me, and in place of dipping early, might want to strike up a good conversation.

2. I'll think about how short life is. This one's really deep, I know, but sometimes I'll be like, "Whoa, Bethany, you don't have all this time in life. You have one life and you should use every second of it." And if I'm focusing my attention on what I could be doing instead of what I *am* doing instead, then how can I possibly enjoy myself? So I'll try to re-ground myself. I'm out for a reason, so I should find what's good about it.

3. I'll do a little self-therapy. It's easy to call a party "lame." You know what's harder? To dig deep and see if the issue is actually more about myself. So if I'm just sitting in a corner, I might ask myself, *"Why am I not having fun? Why am I not socializing?"* Once I pinpoint the reason—most often, it's that I don't know anyone at the party and I feel too shy to break into a conversation—I can deal with it directly. I can introduce myself to one new person, just to see what happens. And sometimes, just one good conversation in a night is enough.

honest compliment. (I will never compliment someone on something that I'm not into.) It seems so silly to start up a hopefully meaningful conversation with something as silly and small as nail polish or a dress, but a genuine compliment can go a long way—and if you *do* like her style, you probably have other interests in common, too. But if you don't click with the person you approach, that's just fine: you could be the person at the party hopping around to make people feel good, like a compliment angel!

Choosing Friends Wisely

Friends have a big effect on your attitude, on how you treat people, and on the thoughts you're having. That's why I work hard to surround myself with people who are motivated, positive, and passionate about life. When I see my friends excited about life or succeeding, it makes me more motivated to accomplish my own goals and dreams. Sometimes, the best thing a solid friend can do is be a good influence on the way you lead your life.

On the other hand, it's also important to recognize when someone in your life is dragging you down. If they are, you can keep them at a distance so you're not spending so much time

RANDOM ME FACT: I DON'T HAVE "BEST" FRIENDS

What I mean by that is I don't *label* them that way. Labels just make things complicated, because then you end up feeling the need to fill a spot or find different terms for everyone, like "That person is just my best friend, but that other person's my *best* best friend." Sometimes I'll use the hashtag #bestie or #bestfriend, but I don't use it as a ranking order. Your friends shouldn't be ranked as a hierarchy; and so, describing someone as my best friend just means I love you, a ton!

with them, and reevaluate how you feel about that person in a month. It's better to have a few quality friends who build you up than a whole gaggle of friends who tear you down bit by bit. I often ask myself these questions if I'm wondering if a friend is right for me.

First I might ask myself, "How do I *feel* around this person?" This is the most important element in a friendship for me. Sure, sometimes you just *know*. You get vibes, whether it's positive or negative energy. But if I'm on the fence about a particular friend, I might ask myself after we've hung out, "Do I feel energetic, motivated, and excited? Or do I feel negative and pessimistic?" Because I've definitely had people in my life who've passed along their bad, toxic energy to me. The minute I leave one of these people, I'll wonder why I'm feeling so horrible—and then I'll realize, it's because my friend was being nothing but

negative the entire time we hung out. (By the way, I'm not talking about friends who are just going through a difficult time—in that case, I'm always there to support them, of course!)

I'll also ask, "What is his or her *intention* as my friend?" Do they care about me for who I am, or is there another motive? I want friends who are going to be good to me, but who also call me out on bad habits and negative actions.

Finally, it's important to ask, "Is my friend encouraging me when I want to pursue something? Or is he or she hindering my growth as a person?" I've had friends who would encourage me to skip my workouts, literally every single day, even though they knew living a healthy lifestyle is important to me. That kind of friend is not someone I want in my corner. Friendships have such a huge impact on my life that I only want positive, caring, encouraging friends by my side.

Dealing with Peer Pressure

When I was growing up, I basically had two close friends. At the time, I felt a lot of pressure to be just like them: We'd try to match outfits and look the same, so we could be a unit. And while that was fun sometimes, I also felt like I was limiting myself. Because even if I wasn't into something the other two liked, I would force myself to "enjoy" it all the same. Thinking back, it's like, how silly is *that*? Dear Young Bethany: #dbd, aka don't be dumb!

The fact is, rather than feeling pressured to do or say or wear or try the same things as your friends, it's better for you all to have varying interests and follow different paths, so you can learn from each other. Yes, I have a lot of friends who make YouTube videos, of course. But I'm also surrounded by amazing women who are all very different from one another. And I love that. There's no pressure for any of us to be the same, and because they work in different industries than I do, we're constantly learning from each other.

I'm Obsessed With . . . My Leather Jacket

If I want to hang out with friends one night, I'm almost always wearing my leather jacket—which I guess is why people are convinced I'm this biker chick, but I'm not! I just really like mine, and I wear it with everything. In a way, my leather jacket has become my security-clothing piece, because it's timeless, and I know that no matter what the trends are, it'll always look good on me.

My go-to is a jacket with a tiny zipper pocket in the front that I got from a Zara in Korea on a whim, but it's since turned out to be my favorite! It fits perfectly and accentuates my curves really well. Here's what I look for in a leather jacket:

Cropped fit: I like them cropped, hitting just below the belly button.

Simple look: Nothing with a lot of buckles or zippers that up the grunge factor.

Soft feel: I love a soft, buttery leather—but if that breaks the budget, then at least go for a thinner leather (or pleather) that will fall more naturally than a thick, stiff one.

Snug fit: I prefer a tailored leather jacket. I feel like some are cut to look baggy and oversized, but I think a snug fit is better.

HANGING WITH MY GRAM

I had a realization recently about my grandmother: "Whoa," I thought, "my grandmother has been on this earth more than three times as long as I have, and she has taught me so much." It made me think about what it was like for her growing up, and wonder about some of the things she knows that I haven't learned yet. And maybe there are even things I know that I could teach her. (For example, I would love for my grandma to have Instagram or try Snapchat. Of course, she would never figure out how to post or use the filters right, so it would be hilarious. But that would be the beauty of it—I love watching people who don't know how to use technology!)

The thing is, my grandma only speaks Portuguese, and so I've never had a full conversation with her. She only knows about ten words in English, and I tried to learn a few words in Portuguese, but bridging that gap is very difficult.

At one point, I asked my dad why he never taught me how to speak Portuguese, and he explained how he was picked on as a kid for speaking the language. Of course, that was a really long time ago and just my dad's experience. (Other people might have a very different one!) But it's why he was afraid my sister and I would get teased, too. (That explains a lot about why parents do things sometimes—even if it may not make sense at the time, it's because of something they themselves have experienced.)

A couple of years ago, though, I started thinking about how unique my relationship with my grandma really is. I've never spoken with her about my day or heard about the things she likes, but we still have a connection. In fact, one of the most genuine hugs I can get is from my grandma, because that's how we express our love for each other—through our body language and energy. It doesn't matter that we can't exchange words, because our hugs are the most important language we have. Sometimes, a connection isn't so much about what you say, but about the love you put out into the world.

Girls' Night Veggie Pizza

Having a girls' night is so important. It's great to hang out, have snacks, sit and talk, and put our phones away—well, for the most part, anyway (come on, we need our phones for some Snapchat!). It feels so good to relax with a bunch of girlfriends who just want to hang out and have a good time.

Cooking for your friends makes the night even more special. One of the easiest ideas is a homemade pizza that everyone can split. This is my favorite veggie pizza combination, but you can customize it with whatever your favorite vegetables are.

SAUCE INGREDIENTS

1 small onion, diced

2 tbsp olive oil

2 cloves garlic, minced

1 (28 oz) can crushed tomatoes

salt and pepper, to taste

¼ cup chopped fresh basil

red chili flakes

PIZZA INGREDIENTS

pre-made pizza shell, ready for baking

1 zucchini, sliced

1 tomato, diced

1 red pepper, sliced in long slivers

1 cup chopped broccoli florets

TO MAKE THE SAUCE

Sauté the onion in olive oil over medium heat for about five minutes, until soft. Add the garlic and sauté for two more minutes. Add the crushed tomatoes, salt and pepper, basil, and red chili flakes. Simmer over low heat for fifteen to twenty minutes, stirring often.

TO MAKE THE PIZZA

Step 1: Preheat oven to 450°F (or whatever temperature is listed on your pizza shell packaging).

Step 2: Spread your homemade pizza sauce all over the unbaked crust, then top with layers of sliced vegetables and the chopped broccoli florets and an extra sprinkle of red chili flakes.

Step 3: Bake for eight to ten minutes, or until the edges of your veggies turn a nice golden brown. Slice up and share with your friends!

6 AWESOME GIRL DATES

Dates aren't just with guys. Once a month—at least—I try to do something different with my girlfriends to bond. Here are some things we'll do.

1. Go hiking. I try to do a lot of fitness things with my friends. It gets us outdoors, keeps us active, and we get to talk about everything under the sun. Though we do always reach a point halfway through the hike where all the talking stops and we're just breathing heavily, because hiking is *hard*!

2. Get a tarot card reading. One friend and I have this tradition where we get tarot card readings and sit in on each other's session. I feel like it's brought us a lot closer because while everything in a reading is not accurate, it gets us talking about our personal lives. I'm telling you, if you want to get to know someone, get a reading done together because it'll bring up all these issues beneath the surface that you can talk about together.

3. Get a couples' massage. No one said you have to be an official "couple" to get one. A friend and I will go to the spa and get massages in the room together. Then we'll go downstairs in our robes, put on our swimsuits, and get in the hot tub. It's relaxing and really fun.

4. Get our nails done. Manicures and pedicures are always more fun with friends. And because you can't be on your phones while getting your nails done, it's a great time to catch up on your lives.

5. Do face masks at home. You can do any kind of spa night at home, but the thing I'll do most often with a friend is a face mask. Then we'll lie down on the bed and talk while the serums sink in.

6. Take a class. Okay, so I haven't actually done this with a friend yet, but I've wanted to for a *really* long time! I just have to schedule it. I want to take a cooking class, or a sushi-making class, or an eating class—if such a thing exists, that would be *awesome*.

Un-Social Is Okay, Too

I used to feel so guilty about being introverted—like it was a bad thing to be shy. But now I know that while I have moments where I genuinely want to engage with people, I also have moments where I just want to be alone. And that's important, too, because we have to recharge!

The more I've socialized, the more I've learned that no one is completely introverted or completely extroverted. We all move back and forth between the two, depending on our mood or the people we're around. So now I no longer feel guilty for those moments when I want to just be with myself. I think a healthy life is about balancing those feelings. Alone or with others, I'm still the real me.

A FUNNY STORY: "I SPEAK KOREAN! SORT OF . . ."

I got to go on a business trip to Seoul, South Korea, to learn all about Korean skincare and beauty. While I was there, my friend Sarah was showing me around the city and taught me a few sentences in Korean because she speaks it fluently.

First, she taught me to say "Hello" and "Thank you," which I used all the time. Then, one night, while we were in one of the twenty-four-hour shopping malls, she taught me how to say, "How much is this?" in Korean. I was so proud of myself for learning the phrase that as soon as I got it right, I went up to the cashiers.

"Hello," I said in Korean. "How much is this? Thank you."

But what I didn't realize is that of course they thought I knew more words than that—so the cashiers started responding to me in Korean! I was just standing there with a blank look on my face and had to say, "Uh, that's it for me . . . that's all I got!"

All of this is to say: the next time I try and "learn" a language in the middle of a mall, I'll try and get past the first seven words!

RANDOM ME FACT: I'M KNOWN FOR BEING A TERRIBLE TEXTER!

Apparently, I take a long time to respond to my friends by text, but it's never intentional—like, I'm never *trying* to wait a day or two to write back. Sometimes I'm just so busy, I don't have time to respond. And since I don't want that blue dot beside my unread messages (it's the worst!), sometimes I'll click on a text without having a chance to respond. And other times, I'll read a message and *think* I responded, and then my friend will call me out on it like, "Uh, hello?!" I just enjoy talking face-to-face more than I do typing a text. Plus, I'm very to the point. If I'm texting, I want to be productive and make plans and that's it.

My Social Media Friends Are My Friends, Too

My social media friends are just as important to me as the friends I see in person. Just because a friendship starts on the Internet, doesn't mean it isn't a real bond. And I know this because of the community that has grown around me: my Motavators.

I never expected that a group of people who started out as my audience could grow to become my friends. More than that, actually: It feels like we're family. Over the years, I've seen some of the same people at my meet-and-greets, and each time, they'll be taller or in high school now, or in college, and I'll feel so proud to see how much they have changed!

Yes, I've been growing up on camera, but they've grown with me. We've been figuring ourselves out together, and I'm so thankful to have their support.

And it's not just the connections I have with my viewers that excite me; it's also the connections they make with each other. I'll see them interact on Twitter and post photos of themselves, and, over time, actual friendships have even formed through my channel. Viewers will tell me all the time, "Hey, we all met because we're Motavators!" and it feels incredible to see what they have built. *That's* what encourages me to make more videos: to keep our community strong.

The other aspect that blows my mind is that a lot of my viewers are from different countries around the world, and through communicating with them, I've seen that even though we live in completely different cultures, we can still be so similar! It's crazy, sometimes: No matter where each of us lives, we might listen to the same music, or like the same makeup, or dress in a similar style. But most of all, we all have the same emotions. It makes the world feel a lot smaller when I think about that.

Some people see social media as negative, but the question I ask is "How are you using it?" Because if you're using social media for good—like I always try to—it's a positive, powerful way to connect with people. For me, it's been even more than that. It hasn't just connected me to my viewers and my Motavators; it's been an instrumental tool in making new friends that feel just like family.

BEHIND THE SCENES: THE FUN OF MY YOUTUBE FRIENDS

I love having friends who work in the YouTube space, because whenever I have a YouTube issue—like if my editing software is messing up or I don't know what I want my next video to be—they get it and can help. I've met most of them at events. For instance, I met Connor Franta at a YouTube party, and Lindsey Stirling at a seminar. I met Troye Sivan at a YouTube event, too, but we had a more unusual experience . . .

Some female YouTubers and I were about to do an onstage performance where we each had to do a male YouTuber's hair, and the audience was going to vote for whose hair was best. Thirty minutes before we were going on stage, though, we still needed one more guy!

When I saw Troye, I thought, "I've seen some of his videos before. I wonder if he would be down?" So I went up to him and said, "Hey, I'm Bethany. Want to do this thing on stage with me?" And he was like, "Sure!" So that's how we met, with me doing his hair on stage!

We didn't win; we got like second place . . . or maybe it was third. (Okay, fine, guys' hair obviously isn't my thing!) But missing out on a win didn't matter to me, since our friendship has lasted ever since.

Hey, Friend-Shifts Happen

When some of my early friendships ended, I remember thinking, "Agh, I thought we were friends for life! What even is a BFF?!" It shook up my belief of what friendships were, and made it harder for me to open up to new people and start building trust all over again.

Compared to dating relationships, friendships can be more casual, but they're still so important. Whether it's a girl friend or a guy friend, it's still a relationship; it's getting to know someone, being vulnerable around them, and spending time together—and time is one of the biggest gifts you can give to someone, because you can't get that back.

To me, the best kind of friend is one who is reliable and who will be there for you, because that's the kind of friend I am. I don't like feeling like I'm always there for a friend if that

RANDOM ME FACT: I'M NOT A FAN OF SMALL TALK.

I find it hard to sustain a lot of small talk; I prefer to talk about something more meaningful with people if I can. So often we fall back on the same old questions and answers, like, "How are you?" "I'm good, how are you?" And it's kind of a waste of energy when, instead, we could be asking each other, "How are you *really* doing?" Or, I'll get more specific and ask, "Anything stress you out today?" I once casually asked one of my friends that question, and she went on for an hour! But it was great; she needed to vent and I felt more connected to her, which is the point. I still sometimes go to the default question of "How are you doing?" just because it's polite. But if a conversation feels too superficial, I prefer to try to get to a deeper place, because that's how you make real friends.

same friend isn't always there for me. Good friends make each other a priority, and love each other for who they are.

At the same time, people can also naturally grow apart. Sometimes you don't even have a fight; you just find that, down the line, you're investing your time in different activities or going to different schools. Sometimes, you can feel someone pulling away, and even if you try and prevent a rift from growing, the other person just isn't invested in fixing it and the friendship fades. I once had a friend who stopped connecting with me, and while I kept trying to keep the friendship going, I eventually reached a point where I felt stupid, like "Hang on, why am I trying if they're not?"

Ultimately, I think growing apart is okay; it's a natural response to our lives changing and evolving. It doesn't always mean forever; it just means you're in different places right now. Ultimately, I think people move in and out of our lives for a multitude of reasons. I think we're meant to have lasting connections with some friends while others are meant to be part of our lives for shorter periods of time as we learn and grow with one another. So I've learned to cherish the people around me and make the most out of the time we have.

I Stopped Comparing Myself to Others

I used to compare myself to other people a lot. I'd think, "I wish I were more like her" or "I wish I had her wardrobe" or whatever. But a couple of years ago, I realized that whenever I wanted to be someone else, it was either for physical or materialistic reasons, rather than *who* she was, inside, as a person.

Here's what I know now: When you say you want someone else's life, that's because you haven't been devoting the work and time you deserve to yourself. You'd feel better about your life if you took active steps to improve it, by setting health or fitness goals, or taking actionable steps toward achieving your career dreams. Of course, it takes time to achieve what you want, but it's more valuable to honor the journey you're on—every small step of the way—instead of coveting what someone else has. And the second you start honoring your own needs and who you are as a person, you'll be committed to being *you* again. I think we'd all be happier if we reminded ourselves, "*This* is the life I'm blessed with. This is who *I'm* meant to be."

8

Dating

{ *You are a complete person, first and foremost.*
Dating someone is just the cherry on top. }

The Nervous Excitement

The feeling of liking someone new is so exciting. You wonder if they like you back, you get giddy to see them, and you do embarrassing things around them . . . or is that just me? (Yeah, it might just be me. I've embarrassed myself so many times!)

But I think the coolest thing about dating is that it's so uncertain. As human beings, we have such a craving for certainty; we always want to know where things fit and what's coming next. But what makes dating fun is that it's the opposite of certainty: It's all about the element of surprise.

My First Kiss

When I was about seven years old, I had a crush on a boy who was a family friend. We hung out all the time, and we were really close. I had a big Barbie tent that I loved to play in, and one day when he came over

we decided to play house. I made popcorn and I was like, "I'm the wife and you're the husband." Then we went into my Barbie tent and pretended to be a married couple. Typical!

We did "chores" while eating the popcorn. And then, halfway through the game, we had a little peck on the lips because, you know, we were married! My parents are still really good friends with his family, but I haven't seen him in years. I love that I have this story to look back on, and I'm grateful my first kiss was playful and super-sweet.

My First Date

Speaking of "firsts," my first date was so weird. I was about fifteen years old, and I liked a different boy I met when I was around seven. We lost touch when I moved away the first time, at age eight, but after I moved back to the area and entered my teens, the boy and I connected on Facebook and started hanging out.

He'd come to my house a lot and he was *so* cute. He was also a year or two older so—hello, he had a driver's license! He seemed so grown up. When he'd come over, we'd hang out in the living room, but it was such a small house that even when my parents were in the kitchen, they could hear everything.

I remember one time he came over and we were trying to watch a movie, but we were so scared to even sit next to each other, so we were sitting five feet apart! We were like sticks, sitting up so straight, pretending to care about this movie when all we could think about was each other. It was all so awkward, but I was totally smitten.

One time, he asked me to go bowling in the next town over. It was about a twenty-minute drive, so my parents didn't want to let me go alone with him. I was so mad, and figured they were obviously insane (as most teenagers think their parents are, of course). Finally they figured out a way I could go: My two boy cousins would just have to come with us. Not great, but better.

So when I finally went on the date, the boy I liked drove and I sat in the front . . . and my two cousins sat behind us in the backseat. It was so weird, but I didn't care, because I was just excited that I got to go at all. All four of us bowled together at the bowling alley (because it would have felt really strange if my cousins were just watching us like chaperones). We all talked and had fun together, and in the end, it was a really good first date experience. I think that group dates are perfect when you first like someone; you're not confined to *just* talking to him or her, so the pressure is off. Plus, it's good to see how someone navigates a social setting and interacts with other people, too.

We went on some other dates after that. I remember when we went to Starbucks, I felt like I was having the greatest time of my life!

We only dated like that for a few months, though, and it was really casual. It's always a weird time when people are graduating from high school and going off to college at different places in the country. With that much distance and all of the new experiences coming your way, you just can't know where a relationship is going to go.

At the time, I was like, "You're gonna be two hours away?! I won't see you anymore!" But in addition to him moving, I was doing YouTube, which meant my schedule was hectic, and I was often working or traveling. So, you know, it just kind of ended. Sometimes it's that simple: It's over. You're okay. And you look forward to seeing who you'll get to meet next.

My 3 Favorite Date Night Looks

There are a few ways I tend to style my hair when I'm going on a date. The last look involves a braid, which I used to think guys saw as a little too young or juvenile, but a lot of my guy friends are fans of braids on girls. All three of these looks make me feel pretty, feminine, and date-ready.

DATE HAIR #1
DOWN WITH A DEEP PART

Step 1: I'll give my hair a lot of volume with a dry shampoo and a texturizing spray, messing it up with my fingers.

Step 2: I create a deep left part with my fingers.

Step 3: For the full side of hair, I'll use my curling wand to add more fullness. I will curl every strand, but with larger sections of hair around the biggest barrel, which creates more of a wave.

Step 4: For the lighter side, I'll curl just a few sections, then tuck the hair behind my left ear. Complete this look with a pair of statement earrings!

DATE HAIR #2
VOLUMIZED PONYTAIL

Step 1: I'll tease the crown with a comb, and sometimes I'll tease my hairline, too. Give your hair as much volume as you can while it's still down.

Step 2: After teasing, I'll use a texturizing spray and mess it up more with my fingers.

Step 3: Sweep it all back into a high ponytail and tie it. If the pony still looks flat or straight in places, I might use my curling wand on a few pieces of hair to add fullness.

Step 4: Sometimes, I'll wrap a little piece of hair around the ponytail to cover the hair band, then pin the piece in place with a bobby pin so it looks classy.

DATE HAIR #3
LITTLE SIDE BRAID

Step 1: I curl my hair with my wand to give it body, using large sections on a big barrel.

Step 2: I create a right part toward the front of my hair. From that right side, I pull a small amount of hair from my hairline into three sections.

Step 3: I French braid those small sections of hair along the hairline, starting at the part and working toward the right ear. (Start with a regular braid, and then, each time you braid a new piece of hair, pull a tiny amount of hair along the way into the braid.)

Step 4: When the French braid reaches the right ear, I tie the braid off with a hair tie and secure the whole piece behind my right ear with bobby pins.

P.S. I ALWAYS GO A LITTLE MESSY WITH MY HAIR ON DATES

I don't like my hair looking too sleek and perfect. Because if it's perfect and then gets tousled in the wind, it's a lot more noticeable. I don't want to worry about my hair during the date; I want to be chill and enjoy myself. So I tend to mess it up before it gets the chance to *get* messed up.

Being Single Is Awesome, Too!

Dating for me is hard. That's partly because I'm always so busy, but mostly because I love being independent!

In recent years, I've been lucky enough to travel all over the world. When I'm experiencing new foods or taking in new sights, I sometimes wish I had someone with whom I could share those places. But at the end of the day, whether I'm dating someone or not, I'm so happy with my life and am focused on growing into the person I want to be. So when I'm single I'm in no rush to start a relationship. I've done a lot of self-improvement over the past couple of years, and I'm giving myself time to figure myself out. That way, when I enter a relationship, I'll know and love myself and won't be looking for a guy to complete me.

I've never liked the idea of someone "owning my heart" or me "giving my heart" to someone. Hello, *I* own my heart. When we find someone we connect with, we give him or her access to our hearts, yes, but each of us is complete on our own. What I want is someone who complements me, someone who can be my partner, like a team player. I never want to feel like I'm not whole without someone else by my side. I want to feel completely me, so that I can be fully present and supportive of someone else.

Plus, there's a reason they call a relationship a commitment. If I'm going to date someone, I want him to be able to lean on me and vice versa. Why do the whole "boyfriend" or "girlfriend" label thing if you can't be there all the time for that person? No one deserves to be shortchanged in love. I like to spend a lot of time with and give a lot of my energy to the person I'm serious about, so if I don't have that time or that emotional space to give him, I'm better off on my own. And that's why I have come to love the single life as much as seeing someone—because this time of self-discovery and learning independence is an important part of growing up.

WHAT I LOOK FOR IN A GUY

Here's how my guy radar used to work: If he was cute, I liked him. If he wasn't my "type," I wasn't into it. But now, a guy's looks aren't the biggest factor. Sometimes I might not find someone initially attractive just by looking at him, but when we sit down to talk, I'll find that my attraction grows. So now I've started to pay attention to different attributes and qualities in guys that are just as important as looks are . . . if not more.

I LIKE A GUY WHO . . . can have an easy conversation. Good conversation is a big deal. I like to hear all about the other person's likes, dislikes, hobbies, and aspirations. And I think what attracts me to someone is if he isn't put off by my interest in his life.

I LIKE A GUY WHO . . . is patient for me to open up. On the other hand, I'm not quick to open myself up to other people—and some guys can take that as being standoffish or cold. But in reality, it just takes me a little while to gain trust in someone else. If I tell someone a little detail about me, I feel like I'm giving up a piece of me—even if all I've told you is my favorite color! Recently, I've been trying to live in a vulnerable state more often, especially when I'm on a date.

I LIKE A GUY WHO . . . has a curiosity for things. I like when a guy craves knowledge in the world. Maybe he's into documentaries or psychology or he likes to go to seminars and study self-growth. If he's always looking to learn more about himself and the world the same way I am, we'll both be able to learn from each other.

HOW I . . . TEXT WITH GUYS

I TEXT RIGHT BACK—if you like him, text him! I know some people can get caught up in games, like playing hard to get, and might think they need to wait before responding to someone they like. But that's silly. (Remember #dbd? We have to remind ourselves: Don't be dumb!) If I like a guy, I try to text right back. (Key word "try," because I'm such a bad texter, there are times I get distracted and it takes me longer!) I don't purposefully delay, because I'm not afraid of showing someone I care. That lets guys get to know who I am, instead of me pretending to be a high-maintenance "hard to get girl" who takes two days to respond.

I'LL SEND UNIQUE PHOTOS OF SOMETHING I DID OR SAW. One time, a guy sent me a photo of something he was doing that day, and I was like, "Oh that's so sweet, he likes me." And then I went on his Snapchat and he'd put the same thing up there for everyone to see! I just think it's more special when you send someone a photo you're not sending anywhere else. So if I like a guy, I might send him photos of something cool I did, or a video I saw—but I'll only send them to him.

I DON'T TRY TOO HARD TO BE FLIRTY. You know when you try to overplay flirty vibes? The overuse of the winky face is a huge indicator. Believe me when I tell you I've added a million winky faces in a row. Well, maybe not a million, but close enough. It's just so easy to get caught up in wanting to show someone you're interested, that saying something really over-the-top sounds like the right move to make. In reality, all it usually does is backfire. And you *know* when you're trying too hard. Like, if I have to sit there and think of a flirty response for fifteen minutes, I know I shouldn't send it—because I never would have been able to think of it fast enough to say it face-to-face in the first place! So if I like someone, I'll write the first thing that comes into my head—which is exactly what I would say if I were actually with the person—and send that. Plus, if you've spent all that time crafting *the* perfect sentence, then you're so much more invested in getting *the* perfect response from your crush (and it's never fun to receive a one-word text that says "nice" after you've just crafted the most beautiful piece of text-poetry . . . or so you thought). So keep it easy: Just type what you feel and send what you'd say!

Love Yourself First

There's nothing worse than liking someone who doesn't like you back—and then over-thinking and overanalyzing every single possible reason why, over and over again. I'm guilty of getting caught up in that, too! But the bottom line is: You cannot *make* some-one like you. And no matter how much I—or you—analyze those confusing texts we're getting, it literally makes *no* difference in the outcome of the relationship. So I can either overthink it or I can stop thinking about it and just go to a movie; it doesn't affect what happens either way. (So . . . one large pop-corn, please!)

Ultimately, I don't let how guys feel about me affect how I feel about myself. Whether he likes me or not, I know my worth. I *know* I'm a valuable person. If I'm single? Great. I

can work on my career and on keeping myself happy. Then, when I'm with someone who's right for me, I can bring all of that to the table. But in the meantime, I will create happiness for myself—because, by the way, when we're happy in a relationship? That happiness we feel is actually coming from *ourselves*.

And let me tell you, it changed everything when I realized that: The positive, happy feel-ings I have when I'm with another person can be felt at any time! I can feel them when I'm hanging out by myself, or if I'm spending time with family or friends. A guy can't just hand me happiness, because *I already have it within me*. That person you're dating isn't the holder of your happiness. *You* are. You are a complete person first and foremost. Dating someone is just the cherry on top.

Where the Boys Are

It's so hard to meet guys sometimes. I mostly meet them through mutual friends or at work events. Recently, I saw the same guy at a few different events and I recognized him, so we started talking. That can be cool because it shows you're in a similar social circle and might have some stuff in common. (He and I then followed each other on Twitter, which

is a big step these days. But that's as far as it went.)

I have a few friends who use dating apps and enjoy them, but I don't. I'm scared of Tinder! I did try a dating app once, but I got more caught up in how fun it was to go through the photos, and didn't want to actu-ally meet the guys!

I think the reason I'm disinterested in Tinder and other dating apps is that so many of the guys are generic or lazy when writing their messages and bios. I got a lot of messages that just said, "Hey," paired with a smiley emoji. I wouldn't respond, because what I really wanted to write was "I *know* you just cut and pasted that to all of your matches."

Some guys are creative, though. My favorite was the time I didn't respond to this one guy for weeks. And then he sent a message that read, "Is this our first fight?" I was like, "Okay, I'll take that!" It was really cute.

When You *So* Don't Like a Guy

I don't like to give my number out. But I used to feel bad telling a guy "No" if he asked for my number, so I tried a few ways to get around it.

One time, I met a guy when I was out with my girlfriends, and he and I struck up a nice conversation. At the end of the day, though, I just wasn't interested in dating him, so when he asked for my number, I panicked and gave him my sister's number on impulse. Later that night, he texted her saying, "Great meeting you," so of course she called me like, "Who just texted me? Did you give someone my number?!" I was like, "I'm sorry!" I told her she didn't have to respond, but I felt really bad about that. Oops.

I've told a few guys that I'd be happy to give them my email address, but they each got really offended, like my email was the lamest thing they could get. Rude.

I've thought about the idea of completely making up a number when a guy asks for my number, but then there's the potential of the guy saying, "Here, let me call you right now so you have mine . . . Wait, why isn't your phone ringing?" And then I'd have to pretend like I'm on airplane mode and really hope someone doesn't answer that other number and . . . well, I just can't see that ending well.

So now here's what I do if I don't want to give my number to a guy: I politely turn him down. I used to think that if someone asked me a question, I had to answer it; and if someone asked for my number, I had to give it. Eventually, I had the realization that other people aren't entitled to our private information. We shouldn't feel pressure to provide guys with our number just because they ask. Now, if I'm not into it, I'll thank a guy for his interest and then say, "No thank you," or "I don't give out my number." And that's all you need to do. Saying no is enough.

A FUNNY STORY:
"OMG, I HAVE GUM IN MY HAIR!"

Once you reach a certain age, you're not supposed to get gum in your hair anymore, right? Well, I guess I'm not there yet because it happened to me recently!

I went to dinner with a guy, and I wasn't sure if it was a date or not, so I wanted to make a good impression. I had on my cross-body bag, and I was walking to his car. As soon as I got in, I went to pull my bag off my shoulder, and I saw this weird white thing stretching from my bag to three different sections of my hair. That's when I realized that, somehow, a piece of my own chewed gum had gotten on the bag strap, and now all my hair was clumped together. I mean, the gum was literally *everywhere*.

As the guy was getting in the car, I didn't want to say anything, because I was embarrassed. And since I didn't want to let on about the gum in my hair, dealing with it was going to seriously complicate my ride! But I was determined to fix it. I didn't need peanut butter or some other gum-removal trick—I was just going to get it out.

The ride to dinner was torturous. Even though he was really into the conversation, I had to "Yeah, yeah" him while both of my hands were in my hair, frantically trying to pull out the pieces of gum and unstick the whole mess. I was working my pull-magic on the window side of the car, and it was dark so, luckily, he couldn't really see what I was doing. And he's lucky, too, because he probably would have been grossed out to know that his date (or not-date) pulled out so much of her hair—literal chunks—in his car. I'm not kidding: My scalp hurt by the time we got to the restaurant.

Before we got out of the car, I put the hair in an empty gum wrapper and then put that wrapper-hair clump in my purse (glamorous, I know). I think I was doing a good job of being like, "Mm-hmm, yes," but I wish I could have been more into his story. I guess next time I'm going to be more careful with how I dispose of my gum—for the sake of my hair *and* love life.

4 WAYS TO GO ON AN "ADVENTURE DATE"

You can go to dinner and the movies, but in my opinion, a date should be something you'll never forget—after all, it could be the start of something special!

MY FAVORITE PICKS:

1. Farmers market. I once brought a guy to my favorite farmers market and it was so cool because I really knew my way around. I proudly introduced him to the vendors I knew, and the guy I was with was super-impressed. It's since become my favorite way to show a date a real piece of my life. What I love about this as a date is that you get to be outside, stroll around and sample the food—and most farmers markets let you enjoy some strawberries and try dips together for free.

2. Amusement park. Growing up, I used to go to Disneyland with my family a lot, so going to an amusement park always takes me back to the feeling of being a kid. I think going to one on a date brings out playfulness in both of you.

3. Picnic. If you have a meal outside, it's like visiting a restaurant that only the two of you know about. Plus, because I'll be dressed more casually for kicking back, I'm more apt to relax and just be myself.

4. A sporting event. Instead of staring at each other and being nervous about making conversation, you can watch the game or event and talk to each other about it between plays.

DIY: Pack a Day Date Picnic Basket

You don't have to go somewhere fancy on your date. If you pack a small lunch, you can go to any park or beach and turn the outdoors into your in spot. Fill a big woven picnic basket with some easy-to-eat food items that don't require utensils or a lot of fuss—and pack these other fun essentials, too:

- A cute blanket to sit on

- 2 cloth napkins

- 2 Veggie Wraps (page 156)

- Veggie Sticks with Sriracha Hummus (page 159)

- Watermelon slices, for a light dessert

- A Polaroid camera, to take fun photos of yourselves on the picnic

- And if your date brings you flowers, bring those along for a pretty centerpiece

THE BEST AND WORST DATE FOOD!

I'm a very messy eater, so I have to be extra careful of what I order if I'm going on a date. Beware of anything that takes a long time to chew, for example, because when you're on a date, time feels very amplified, so that two seconds can feel like twenty! So now I know what to order and what to avoid.

I'LL EAT . . .

- Sashimi, miso soup, and edamame. The only items I'll order at a sushi restaurant on a date are the ones I can eat easily in one bite, with no drama. Unless you accidentally pop out an edamame bean and hit him in the face. Which I almost did once. Go me.

- Penne pasta. Or any type of pasta that you can just stab with your fork. Getting a long pasta—like spaghetti—is risky because you might splash yourself with the sauce while you're trying to twirl a bite onto your fork.

I WON'T EAT . . .

- Sushi rolls. I was once hanging out with a guy friend of mine when I put a whole piece of roll in my mouth. The seaweed was so chewy, and the two minutes I spent trying to eat it were so awkward! So now I'm terrified of eating sushi rolls on a date.

- Salad. I love salad, but I always get pieces of lettuce stuck in my teeth. I suppose it could be a way to figure out if he's a keeper or not, though, because I really respect someone who has the confidence to tell me when I have something in my teeth.

Veggie Wrap

INGREDIENTS

2 whole wheat wraps

6 tbsp hummus

½ cup cooked brown rice

½ cup black beans

½ an avocado, sliced

½ a red bell pepper, sliced into slivers

½ cup chopped raw broccoli

½ lemon

salt and pepper, to taste

TO MAKE THE WRAPS

Step 1: Lay out both wraps and the rest of the ingredients.

Step 2: Spread 3 tbsp of hummus on each wrap to hold ingredients together. Then, layer one half of the following ingredients on each tortilla in this order: brown rice, black beans, avocado slices, red pepper, and a sprinkle of chopped broccoli. Squeeze lemon onto both wraps, then season with salt and pepper.

Step 3: Roll up the wraps and slice each in half, placing each in a separate glass food storage container.

Veggie Sticks with Sriracha Hummus

If you like spicy flavors (like I do!), this is a great combination of crunchy, refreshing vegetables dipped in a slightly spicy sauce.

INGREDIENTS

- **container of hummus**
- **1 tbsp sriracha hot sauce**
- **red chili flakes**
- **½ tsp olive oil**
- **carrot sticks (or baby carrots)**
- **celery sticks**
- **red bell pepper slices**

TO MAKE THE HUMMUS

Step 1: Scoop a container of hummus (either plain or flavored with herbs or sesame seeds) into a bowl.

Step 2: Add the sriracha (and more if you can take it!) and a sprinkle of red chili flakes into the hummus. Blend with a spatula, top with olive oil, and sprinkle more red chili flakes on top.

Step 3: Transfer your spicy hummus into your container. Dip the veggie sticks into the hummus for a *hot* date.

Talking to Guys on a Date

Dating can be really fun, but it can also be kind of stressful because you never know what's going to happen. Before every date, I usually think, "Is it going to be awesome? Is he going to be great? Or am I going to want to leave halfway through?" Here are a few things I've learned will keep the conversation going and help me figure out if I like him.

- I ask big questions. One of my favorites is to find out what really gets him excited about life. I'll ask, "What would you be doing for work if you weren't doing what you're doing now?" or "What hobbies are you most passionate about?" It's a really cool way to break the ice while also taking the conversation to a slightly deeper level.

- I don't hide who I am. I'm getting better at not hiding my likes, dislikes, and quirks at the beginning of a relationship. Because how long can you spend with someone and continue to hide the stuff you don't want the other person to know? They're going to find out who you are eventually, so it's better to lay it all out right away. Even the stuff you're insecure about—just own it. Because a guy who can't accept you for who you are isn't worth your time, anyway.

- I really listen to the other person. We tend to be so focused on ourselves when we meet someone that we forget to actually *listen* to what the other person is saying. You'll find yourself feeling more relaxed and connecting more with the other person if you're invested in their response. If you ask questions you really want to know the answers to, you will be more engaged with what they say.

- I enjoy the silence. Some people think silence is awkward and they should fill every second. But it says a lot if you can be comfortable in silence with someone. Like, if you're with your mom, or siblings, or closest friends, you can sit quietly for hours, and it's not awkward, right? So if you're with someone and nervously searching for what to say, try to accept the silence instead. We don't have to be speaking every single second.

- Instead of asking "Does he like me?" I ask, "Do *I* like *him*?" Anytime I've found myself asking, "Am I doing this right?" I have to remember the most important question of all: Does he deserve me? We choose who we spend our time with . . . so why choose someone we feel like we have to constantly impress? Do we really want to be with someone if we're always second-guessing ourselves? It's not all about the guy. It's key for me to remember that *I'm* important, too. My personality, my thoughts, and my desires should come first, and if he fits into that, great. If not, there will surely be someone else who will.

- I find the best in the situation. Even if a date doesn't work out, it can still be a positive experience. Maybe you'll learn a few things, or maybe the person will turn out to be a really good friend. Love connection or not, I always try to find the good, because our experiences only help shape our future.

SO EMBARRASSING: "I GOT BUSTED BY GOOGLE ON MY PHONE"

Okay, so you know how when you're interested in someone, you stalk them online a little bit (or a lot a bit)? Well, I was sort of doing that with a guy I liked. He had mentioned a party he'd gone to the night before, so I Googled photos of him at the party that other people were posting. No big deal, right?

Well, later that day, we were hanging out and he needed to look something up on Google, but he'd left his phone behind. So he was like, "Can I use your phone?"

"Okay," I said, and I gave him my phone. It happened so quickly I didn't realize what was going on. But as soon as he opened up Google, there they were: photos of him I had Google-stalked earlier! The fact that I was spying on him was embarrassingly obvious.

He smiled, and I walked away *so* mortified while he carried on with his search on my phone, but I just kept thinking, "Oh my god, of *course* this happened to me. Of *course* he had to go to Google!" You read that right, guys. I walked away while he still had my phone . . . so I had to go back and collect it from him. It just doesn't get any better!

I didn't mention it then or since, and he never did either. We're still friends now and I laugh about it to myself. But if we talked about it today, I would just own it. I mean, we *all* cyber-stalk our crushes in one way or another, right? We may as well get a good laugh over it!

Getting
CHILL

*How I feed my soul with
alone time and a happy home*

I used to rely on other people for my happiness. Everyone else's mood would rub off on me; whatever someone else said, I believed. Now I know that other people aren't the holders of our happiness—we are! And that's why it's so important to have a great relationship with yourself, and spend time alone with your own thoughts—and doing so in a space at home that reflects the *true* you is one of the best feelings in the world.

9

Me Time

It's important to build a friendship with yourself.

I Used to Be Bad at Chilling Out

I'm a very black-and-white person: I am either super-passionate about something or I don't want to deal with it, and sometimes, it's hard for me to find a middle ground.

So back when I first started working, I became obsessed; I worked all the time. And if I tried to decompress and have fun by going to a movie with friends, I'd be like, "Oh, there goes my career. I'm so unmotivated, I'm not even working!" I know it sounds weird, but I think I got scared that if I pulled back from my work, I might stop caring about it. And

since I wasn't able to relax when I took breaks, I didn't see the point of going out if I was just going to feel guilty the whole time.

The problem was, I was working so much— creating videos, doing business collaborations, recording music, always planning my next steps—that I was burning out. I wasn't enjoying it as much because it was *all* I was doing.

Now I make a conscious decision to let go, because I know that giving myself a chance to unwind and recharge is sometimes just as important as working.

GO ON A ME-DATE!

I like to take myself on dates. Some people think it's weird to go out alone, but I embrace it! It's important to build a friendship with yourself: No matter what happens—in a month from now or a year from now; if you're in a really great relationship or just ending one—you'll always be capable of taking care of yourself. If you like hanging out with *you*, you will always be content.

The hardest part about doing things alone is just getting over that stigma that if you're eating lunch by yourself, people are probably looking at you (when they're really, truly, probably not!). I think it's good to get away, relax and recharge, and just be with your thoughts.

My favorite dates to take myself on are:

1. Go to the movies by yourself. This one is the easiest, really, because you're just hanging out in a dark room anyway! I get popcorn, and find I can pay attention to the movie even better if I'm alone.

2. Get your nails done. I'll get a manicure and pedicure on my own. You can relax and really be present when it's just you.

3. Take yourself out to lunch. I mean, I wouldn't get a *big* table. I'll either pick a table with two chairs, or I'll sit at a sushi bar. And if I get antsy, I always have my phone with me so I can do some creative brainstorming, or I'll bring a book—old-school style.

4. Hit a workout class on your own. Sometimes I'll do SoulCycle with my friend, but sometimes I'll just go alone and really focus. (Now that I know how the class works and I'm not embarrassing myself anymore!)

I *So* Need Alone Time

I have a lot of friends who can't handle alone time because not having someone to talk to will drive them crazy. But I love it. We're so surrounded by opinions and noise around us *all the time*, that it's really easy to forget your inner voice. And yet, it's that voice that's going to guide your whole life.

Every day, it's important for my emotional well-being that I fit in at least five minutes to myself—not five minutes on the computer, or watching TV, or Snapchatting, but five minutes where I am literally just closing my eyes, or lying on the couch quietly, or meditating; five minutes where I'm allowing myself to be at one with my thoughts.

It's kind of scary, though. Because when you have those moments alone, you're very vulnerable and you sometimes reveal thoughts and feelings to yourself you don't mean to, let alone want to broach with a ten-foot pole. For instance, I might realize that the reason I haven't yet called someone back is because I'm scared of making the wrong decision for work, or afraid of saying the wrong thing on the phone. Getting to the root of the truth like that can affect your ego. In fact, I believe the act of confronting the most vulnerable parts of ourselves is one of the reasons people don't like being alone. But the more you spend time with yourself, the better the choices you'll make about everything in your life.

HOW I . . . MEDITATE

Something I really like to do is a short meditation. I'll close my eyes for five or ten minutes and focus on how my body feels. With my eyes closed, I will silently talk myself through all the areas on my body: *I feel my body on this chair . . . I feel my hands on my lap . . . I feel my feet on the floor.* It brings me back to center and grounds me.

We don't realize how infrequently we sit quietly, with only ourselves. Tuning into my body like this really helps lower my stress. Plus, if I have a specific decision to analyze—in my love life or work—meditation helps me get a better perspective on it without having *other* people tell me what to do or how to feel. Instead, I'm able to come up with my own answers because I've been able to really hear myself.

We're the Boss of Our Emotions

I've written a lot about the difficult period of my life when I was dealing with being bullied and feeling down about myself. At the time, having the support of my family was important. But it was also important that they didn't try to *fix* my problem. As great as my family is, they couldn't change how the bullying affected me emotionally. If a hurtful experience cuts you deep, the only person who can fix it is you.

I first turned to YouTube to escape how the bullying was negatively affecting my emotions; putting my energy into creating videos really helped me overcome a lot. But it was, on some level, just a distraction. Because instead of sorting out what was going on with me, I was still tethered to *other* people's emotions and to words *other* people said online. Essentially, I put my happiness in other people's hands. And it went beyond what people said about me online. For example, if one person complimented me that morning, I'd feel great for hours; but if they were unkind for a minute, I'd feel terrible all day. It's easy to blame a teacher or a job or a rude salesperson for making us unhappy. But at the end of the day, we're victimizing ourselves by thinking that way.

Getting through my bullying experience taught me to take my power back. Now I know that I am in control of my happiness.

That means sometimes I may want to wallow on the couch all day with takeout to get out my sad feelings and move on; other times, I'll actively choose to turn my unhappy and anxious thoughts around for the better.

Take it from me: If you're relying on other people to make you feel joyous, or upbeat, or alive, you'll be riding a never-ending roller coaster of emotions that isn't in your control. Of course, if you have a mood or psychological disorder like depression or anxiety, you can't just "snap out of it," but you *can* take proactive steps to get yourself the help you need. The point is, you aren't helpless. You have the power to walk away from that salesperson or bad friend. You have the prerogative to take the steps to quit your job and find a career that will excite you. And if you can't change the circumstance, you can certainly change your perspective.

So instead of looking at a situation as something happening *to* you, look at it as something that is happening *for* you. When I was younger, the bullying was happening *to* me; but I was able to turn it into something positive *for* me: I started my YouTube channel as a way to escape, and look where I am now. You can choose to make the most out of any situation. Your thoughts and feelings are in *your* hands. You are the holder of your own happiness.

My 4 Lazy Hair Hacks

If I don't feel like putting a lot of work into my hair but still want to look cute when I'm home zenning out, I use these four shortcuts.

HAIR HACK #1: CURL THE PONY

The loose curl gives you a softer look that's really easy to pull off.

Step 1: Do a ponytail a bit higher than normal and divide it into three or four big chunks.

Step 2: Curl each of the chunks with a curling wand.

Step 3: Remove the hair tie to release the pony. You'll now have a few pieces of curly hair that will give it a bit of body in just the right places.

HAIR HACK #2:
MAKE BABY SIDE BRAIDS

This spices up plain hair without putting much work into it.

Step 1: With your hair down, grab two small, even sections just at the temples on either side

Step 2: Braid each small section into a tiny braid.

Step 3: Fasten the two braids together with bobby pins on the back of your head. It looks cute and clean.

HAIR HACK #3:
DO A FRONT-ONLY FIX-UP

This creates the illusion that you've done your hair, because the front looks good.

Step 1: Wash just the front portion of your hair, along your hairline—just lean over the sink and splash water on however much or little hair you want to style.

Step 2: Bend over and blow-dry that part upside down to give it a lot of height.

Step 3: Flip your head back over and voilà: Your hair suddenly looks like you've done the whole thing.

HAIR HACK #4: HIDE THE BUMP PONY

This makes any ponytail more voluminous, instead of flat and tired.

Step 1: Take a small section of hair—the same amount you'd use if you were going to wear your hair half-up—and tie it up into a tiny ponytail with a small hair tie.

Step 2: Make sure the tiny pony has volume by pulling, tweaking, and teasing it.

Step 3: Pull the rest of your hair up, pulling the hair *over* the tiny pony to disguise it. Smooth out the hair so you are completely hiding the tiny pony, and then tie off your new, big ponytail. Voilà: You get a full pony, but with more volume.

My "Beth Thoughts" Journal

I have a folder on my computer called "Beth Thoughts" that's basically my journal. I'll type a bunch of thoughts on my Pixelmator app, screenshot it, and save it to the folder.

And I write in all sorts of ways. Sometimes I'll do mini poems, and sometimes I can go for pages and pages speed-writing. It doesn't always make sense, but it feels good to get it down on paper and out of my mind.

One thing I'll also do is take an issue in my life and fantasize that it's someone *else's* story. So, say it's an issue in my love life, like getting mixed signals from a guy: I will take the problem I'm going through, turn it into a story about a different girl having that problem, then I'll change the ending however I want. Because now that it's "fictional," I can make things up and add scenes that haven't happened. It's a good release of energy, with a lot more happy endings.

Reading back what I write also helps me understand my feelings more. I'll often read what I've written right after, but sometimes I'll go back and re-read it later. It's funny to pull journal entries from over a year ago and see what I was writing. Sometimes, I can't help but think, "I was so torn up about *that* guy? I don't even remember his name!"

And that's one of the coolest parts: journaling puts what I'm going through in perspective. When I read about a stressful issue I had in the past that I *never* think about now, it's a reminder that my current problem probably won't be a big deal down the line either. So I stop beating myself up about it and I let a natural solution unfold like it's supposed to.

MY TOP 5 NAPTIME SONGS

These instantly create a chill, nap vibe for me:

- "One" by Ed Sheeran
- "Fast Car" by Tracy Chapman
- "Alesund" by Sun Kil Moon
- "Poison & Wine" by The Civil Wars
- "O" by Coldplay

How I . . . Get Happy

As happy as I am, I still have bad days when I'm running late, or I can't find my wallet, or someone cuts me off on the freeway and I'm stuck behind a granny driver for ten miles—and of course, those things always seem to happen all in a row! But now I have ways to flip my emotions around to work *for* me. Here are the things I use most to turn a bad situation around.

1. I think about all the things I'm grateful for. It might sound cheesy, but if I'm stuck in traffic and really annoyed, I'll go through the list of what I'm grateful for. Like, "I have a car. And it can take me somewhere. And I have a full tank of gas when not everyone can go get a full tank of gas. And I have an amazing family. And I'm on my way to a dinner with a friend." Because what's your other option? To look for more negative things to make you more mad? Why would you want to be angrier? Instead, you can start a domino effect of positive thoughts.

2. I'll do karaoke by myself. This is going to sound so weird, but I will sing Disney show tunes in my car. I'll look up the karaoke version on YouTube then put on my Broadway voice. Like, "For the next three

minutes, I am no longer Bethany Mota . . . I am Ariel!" And then the people in the cars next to me look at me like I'm crazy, but I don't care. I visualize what it would be like to be in a scene, I act it out, and it shifts my mood instantly.

3. I'll think about a moment that was funny. I'll try to think of an embarrassing or funny thing that's happened to me recently, which gets me genuinely laughing out loud—and then, of course, I start laughing because I'm laughing by myself and probably look ridiculous! But all of it shifts my energy into a new mood.

4. I'll change my posture. Slumping makes you feel defeated. So when I'm having a bad day, I take on a posture of confidence instead: I sit up a little taller and pull my shoulders down and hold my chin up, and it changes everything.

5. I jump up and down. Okay, I know I've mentioned a million times in this book already that I do this, but that's because I've probably *used* it a million times! It's my cure-all for so much. In the case of a bad mood, I put on a fun, upbeat song like

"Geronimo" and just bounce up and down like I'm at a rock concert.

6. I'll do my hair and makeup even if I'm not planning to leave the house. Some days when I'm just editing my YouTube videos at home I still get all primped, just for me. I think it's important to do things like this for yourself.

7. I ask, "Will this help me grow?" Most often when I'm in a downer situation, I realize the answer is "Yes"—even if something is just teaching me patience or persistence. There are very few times where the answer is "No." Once I see those opportunities to grow, I immediately become more engaged in the process.

MY 6 FAVORITE WAYS TO RELAX

Of course it's easy to relax when you're getting a massage at a spa. But I also have ways I make my home feel like a spa so I can relax there. I'll:

1. Make herbal tea. I like Sleepytime tea, and I drink it plain, without honey or sugar in it.

2. Read a book in bed. When I relax with a book before bed, I sleep so much better.

3. Turn the lights down and light candles. I like to create a vibe that feels kind of romantic, even if it's just for me.

4. Fill up my bathtub and take a bubble bath. I love going to Lush and getting one of their Bubble Bars for a hot bath.

5. Watch a movie on my laptop. I love watching chick flicks when I'm stressed out, as cheesy as that is. I've probably seen *Love, Rosie* three times; it gets your hopes up about love a little bit, and it's so cute.

6. Play soothing music. I'll listen to classical music. Or, I have a naptime playlist I find really soothing to listen to. I put it on Spotify, and it's public, so you can listen to the whole thing if you want to take a nice long nap. (See my top five on page 171.)

PHONE GOALS: I'M TRYING TO CHILL ON PHOTO POSTING

I used to feel like I had to document everything that I did. If something was a trending activity, or I visited a popular vacation spot, I felt like I couldn't enjoy it if I didn't take a photo and post it online. And if I did take pictures but they weren't great, I'd be so bummed out about it (even if I had the best time ever!). Sometimes I even felt like I was only going places so I could show other people that I had gone there.

Now I'm trying something new: to document a little less and actually live life a little more. The first time I went to a cool coffee shop and the beach and didn't document the whole thing, I was like, "Wow, I still had a great time, even though no one on social media saw it!"

I don't think it's a bad thing to document the things you do. But we can't constantly be concerned about what our lives look like to other people. It's more important to enjoy our lives while they're happening and be in the moment.

Me, Having the Best Sick Day Ever!

Whenever I was sick as a child, I used to eat those popsicles that came in pairs that you'd pull apart. I only liked the root beer–flavored popsicles in the pack, so our freezer was filled with them.

Even today, if I have a fever and I'm feeling super-hot, I love to turn to popsicles. I'll get a box of organic, whole-fruit strawberry lemonade popsicles to cool me down. It's a way to make the most of a bummer situation when I have a lot of things to do and my body is being very rude.

If I'm really sick, I won't feel like getting up and showering right away, so I'll make myself some hot chamomile tea or an herbal berry tea. Then I'll lie in bed with a tray of all the things I need, like my tissues, my cough drops, and my thermometer—because, you know, I have to check my temperature every five minutes to see if the fever has broken, because I'm so ready to get out of bed!

Sometimes, after I make some hot lemon water (which I'm obsessed with), I'll take my sheet and put it over my head, then I'll lean my head over the cup so all the steam goes into my nose. If I have the energy, I'll hop in the shower and turn it on super-high to steam myself out. Feeling fresh is the key to getting better, so I will use a citrusy body wash in the shower. I may do the neti pot thing, which helps with my sinuses but always feels weird.

I also change my clothes a lot when I'm sick, to feel fresh—it never feels good to sit in the same gross clothes day after day. I wear crop tops with a pair of baggy sweatpants. I also wear slippers, like my pair of soft black boot slippers with rainbow speckles, that make me feel cozy. And I wear socks sometimes—you know the fuzzy ones that are shea butter–infused so when you take them off, your feet are really smooth? They're the best.

When it comes to food, I go for items with a ton of water in them. Last time I was sick, I ate a lot of citrus fruit; I went through an entire container of pre-peeled tangerines and ate a lot of cantaloupe. Or I'll make a light vegetable soup for lunch and dinner. Then I watch Netflix on my laptop or lie down and listen to music. I just try to let myself enjoy the rest and make the best of it, because as much as your mind wants you to move, sometimes your body just puts its foot down.

My Perfect Sick-Day Soup

When I'm sick, I love to make a vegetable soup with a light broth. This soup is full of so many nutrients that will help your body heal, and the potatoes are filling without weighing you down. It's also very soothing, making it great for a rainy day when you're just relaxing, too.

INGREDIENTS

2 tbsp olive oil

1 carrot, chopped

1 onion, chopped

1 potato, cut into small cubes

1 rib of celery, sliced into half-moons

salt and pepper, to taste

red chili flakes

1½ 32 oz (48 oz total) cartons vegetable stock or broth

1 tomato, cut into chunks

1 zucchini, quartered lengthwise then sliced into chunks

1 cup of kale, chopped

TO MAKE THE SOUP

Step 1: Sauté the carrot, onion, potato, and celery in the olive oil over medium low heat, adding salt and pepper and a sprinkle of red chili flakes. Cook until the vegetables are soft, about ten more minutes.

Step 2: Add vegetable stock and bring to a boil, then simmer for ten minutes.

Step 3: Add the tomato and zucchini and simmer for five more minutes. Add more salt and pepper here, if desired.

Step 4: Just before you're ready to eat, add the kale and cover for another three minutes. Eat right away, while it's hot, and throughout the day as needed to stay hydrated and feel better!

Traveling in Style

When I used to travel on road trips with my family, there was only one thing I needed: my CD player. It was the big kind of player where you put in the CD and snapped it shut, then listened with those little foam headphones. I had a whole collection of CDs that I kept in one of those zippered cases.

Now I carry a bit more with me, as my travel is usually part-work and part-vacation, all mixed up into one. But I've narrowed it down to only what I need. Here's what my journey looks like:

Style: My go-to outfit is a pair of high-waisted black yoga pants, a soft crop top T-shirt with a cozy cardigan over it, sneaker wedges, and a messy top knot bun.

Baggage: I bring what I call my "secret detective" carry-on suitcase that has four rolling wheels that can go in any direction and makes walking through the airport easy. I also have a matching larger bag that I can check.

Change of clothes: I always have one change of clothes in my carry-on for a long flight, just in case my luggage gets lost and I need a nice outfit for a meeting right after the flight.

Cashmere blanket pillow: One of the best investments I've gotten for traveling is my Ralph Lauren creamy white cashmere pillow that unzips to become a cashmere blanket. You can only use it as one or the other (a pillow or a blanket), but I love it because it's like a piece of home on the road.

Self-help book: I always have a book in my carry-on—preferably a self-help book. (See my list of favorite books on page 194.) I love watching movies on planes, but I try not to give in to the mindlessness of watching the screen the whole time. A book keeps me away from that.

Snacks: I always bring my own snacks. I'll usually grab three individual bags of roasted, unsalted almonds, as well as an apple, an orange, a banana, and maybe a bag of the organic Jelly Belly jelly beans.

Makeup wipes: You know those Josie Maran Bear Naked wipes I use to clean my face at night? I bring them in my travel bag, too, in the mini travel size. Because if I'm going to be sleeping on a long flight, I want to remove all of my makeup as soon as we take off.

Sheet masks: I'll do a sheet mask on really long flights, because flying makes my skin feel super-dry—but sometimes I scare people! When I went to Dubai, I did a Snapchat where I was playing all these songs with my weird white sheet mask on. It was hilarious.

Mini makeup bag: I carry mascara, a lip balm, and a brow pencil so that if I've taken my makeup off but I'm landing at my destination midday, I can still make myself look put together.

My purse: This is where I keep all my essentials that I will keep on me during the flight, like my passport, wallet, phone, and charger.

MY BIGGEST TRAVEL MUST-HAVE: HEADPHONES

If I'm walking through the airport or sitting on a loud, busy flight, sometimes I start to feel more stressed out than I need to. I have the power to change that feeling for myself if I'm always prepared with noise-blocking headphones and something to listen to.

I usually go with my Beats Bluetooth headphones; I find that in-ear headphones will fall out, and over-the-ear headphones have wires that can get tangled and caught up in my stuff.

As for what I listen to, if I'm reading a book or a script on the flight, I like to have an instrumental playing in my headphones while I read. If I'm going on a long flight, I'll also have an audiobook or a fellow YouTuber's podcast downloaded and ready to go.

10

Home

{ I love choosing decor that reflects my personal style and makes me feel good. }

My Room Used to Be So Messy

Growing up, I was really messy. All of my books and paperwork were everywhere. I got all my homework done, but no one could understand how, because I was the only one who knew where everything was!

I remember one time, when I was five or six, my room was such a mess that my mom was like, "That's it. You need to clean your room." Apparently, I got so mad, I stomped around the room refusing to clean it up.

Well, the next thing I knew, I was lifting my foot from underneath a big pile of papers and staring at a pencil that had jabbed into my sole and was just dangling off of me—it was in so deep that even while I was trying to shake it off, the pencil was just hanging off my body! I still have a scar from it. Way to go, messy Beth.

Now I can only work in a clean space. Even if I can't see a mess but I know it's there, lurking in the next room, I'll be distracted, and can't come up with good ideas. And my pencils? They're stored safely on my desk . . . far away from my feet.

My Home Decorating Style

I've always loved decorating my space, even when I was young. I have so many fond memories of decorating my childhood bedroom. I think that's where I get my love of interior design from—decorating that small space that belonged to me and me alone!

For one thing, I always had about ten posters in my room, tacked up all over the walls. Some featured stars of whatever TV shows I was into at the time, but most of them were posters of Britney Spears or *NSYNC that I got from teen magazines like *J-14*.

I was also into really bold colors. For a few years, I loved everything purple and wanted all-purple bedding. Then I wanted this horrifying, green-and-blue abstract polka-dot patterned bedding, and had feather boas in different colors hanging from the walls. And one year, I begged my parents for one of those canopies that hangs from the ceiling and cascades above your bed like a tent.

As a teenager, I wanted everything my sister, Brittany, had. So when she got a bulletin board, of course I was like, "*I need a bulletin board in my room.*" When I got one, it became the center of my small universe. I pinned up concert tickets, photos of me with my friends, and little inspirational quotes. Something about that bulletin board made me feel so grown up.

My taste has changed drastically since my "purple everything" days, but I still love to decorate. I love choosing the colors on the walls, the art, and even the small pieces to put on the nightstand. I love choosing decor that reflects my personal style and makes me feel good.

Living Room Inspo:
What I Love About My Living Room

My living room is one of the happiest places in my apartment. Here's what I love most about it.

- My neutral comfy couch. I just *see* my couch and I get happy, because I've decorated it in colors and textures that make me want to dive into it at the end of a long day. It's a Restoration Hardware white cloud couch, and when you lie on it, it hugs you everywhere. It's softer than my bed! I think it's best to get a couch in a neutral color, like white, beige, or light gray. A real piece of furniture is such a big investment, and if you buy one in a neutral color, you don't run the risk of getting stylistically sick of it, because you can switch up the look with pillows.

- Tons of throw pillows. I have a lot of medium-sized pillows and a few larger pillows that I switch out. I have some in muted colors, like cream, some in Moroccan prints, and some in mixed textures, like knitted ones. For the winter holidays, I'll add pillows with a pop of red or a shimmery silver to reflect the season.

- A couple of throw blankets. You can never have too many blankets. Mine are an indulgently soft gray, which I drape over the back of the couch—because a few layers of snug and comfy are always better than one.

- A fluffy rug. I have a furry white rug spread out under the couch. It's luxurious and cozy.

- A coffee table with an open space below it. I use the opening underneath to fit more pillows that I'll pull out if I have friends over.

DIY: Make Boho Fringe Art

The best way to put the finishing touches on a room you love is by hanging your own unique art. This piece is the comfiest-looking one I've ever made, as it adds texture to your wall by combining the natural elements of soft wool and wood. You can either use a few bright colors of yarn, or you can stay neutral with a few shades of beige—whatever suits your design taste.

WHAT YOU'LL NEED

A length of wood (you can use a twig from outdoors, some driftwood from the beach, or a wooden dowel); wool yarn in around four different colors; scissors; a tape measure; and a pen or pencil for marking off measurements.

HOW TO MAKE IT

Step 1: Using the tape measure, measure the center of your wood and mark it with a pencil. Then equally mark the other spots where you'd like to change to different colors. Plan to leave space on either end yarn-free so you can show off your pretty piece of wood.

Step 2: Unwind one long piece of yarn (the color you want in the center) and drape it over the wood. Adjust the dangling end of the yarn until you find a length that works for your design. Cut this piece with your scissors. (Better to be longer than you want at this point, rather than shorter.) Measure the full length of this yarn and write it down.

(continued)

Step 3: Knot this cut piece around the wood as follows: Fold the yarn piece in half again, so you have one looped end and two free ends. Drape the looped end of the yarn under the center mark on your wood. Then, above the wood, push two fingers through the loop and pull the two dangling ends through it, so the knot is on the bottom.

Step 4: Now, pre-cut more pieces of yarn (about fifty pieces will get you started to keep the project moving swiftly). If you like the length you've knotted, pre-cut your yarn pieces to that same length. (You will cut the design into the bottom of the art later.)

Step 5: Knot away! Knot each piece of yarn, one by one, along the entire length of the wood in the color pattern you like, pulling each piece close together as you go so there are no spaces along the wood. If you run out of yarn, cut and knot more pieces as needed until your design is your desired length.

Step 6: When your knotting is complete, tie one final, long piece of yarn around each end of the piece, which you can use to hang on a nail on your wall.

Step 7: Hang your piece. Then, using the scissors, cut the bottom of the yarn into the pattern you like. If you love the arrow look like I do, with a long point at the center, use your measuring tape to find the center again and cut diagonally up evenly on both sides from there. And that's it! Fringy, boho, beautiful.

MY CHILL-AT-HOME STYLE

When I'm hanging out alone, I'm probably wearing:

- Stretchy shorts or yoga pants
- A comfy graphic T-shirt
- My glasses
- A topknot bun

HOW I... DO MY MESSY TOPKNOT

When I'm wearing my topknot at home, I usually just throw it up and don't think about it. But sometimes I'll put a little more effort into it.

In those cases, I'll sprinkle volumizing powder in my hair and run my fingers from root to tip, then tease it a bit with a comb to add volume. (My hair is kind of thin, so without any help it sits as a limp, small ball on top of my head—which is why I never used to wear my hair in buns! Teasing the hair first builds a bigger, better knot.) Then I'll either messily pull it up on top of my head, or I'll throw my head upside down and pull it together that way and secure it. Every once in a while, I'll pull a few tendrils of hair out from over my ears, or I'll tie a scarf into a knot on the top of my head so the ends of the scarf pop up and look really cute. It's my favorite simple at-home hair . . . that still looks cute enough for a quick Snap.

DIY Mason Jars for Every Room

Mason jars are my favorite thing to DIY. Actually, Mason jars are just my favorite thing, period. They're perfect for organization, and they're a blank slate for your creative imagination. Here's how I use them all around the house.

Living Room: Pour sand into the bottom third or bottom half of the jar. Then add a votive candle and light it (preferably seaside-scented). Beachy bliss!

Kitchen: Fill the Mason jar with cold water, then add cut sprigs of rosemary, basil, or thyme to it, as if it's a vase, and place by the sink. It looks pretty and smells like a garden.

Bathroom: Fill three-quarters of the jar with glass beads. Stick the handles of your makeup brushes into the beads to hold the brushes up.

Office: Paint the rim of the glass jar with a different pop of color for each writing tool. For example: paint a hot pink rim for your pencils, blue for your pens, and yellow for your markers.

I'm Obsessed with . . . My Office Twinkle Lights!

I have loved twinkly tiny fairy lights for years, and I've hung them throughout my house—sometimes in my bedroom or living room, and always in my office. They give the room a relaxing, dreamy vibe. In my workspace, I've sometimes added cute photos onto the light string with wooden clothespins. I've also put twinkle lights in a ball inside a Mason jar (just hide the rest of the cord behind the jar) so that when you dim the lights, they look like pretty fireflies floating inside.

My Bookshelf Style

A bookshelf is the one spot in your home where you can display everything you love—and love to look at—in one perfect place. Here's what I put on mine:

Books. Obvious, I know. But I don't keep all my books on my bookshelf. There are also usually a few books on my coffee table, one on my floor, one in my bag . . . literally everywhere.

Flameless candles. I have about eight and they're on a remote, so I can set them up to stand still, flicker slow, or flicker fast, depending on the vibe I want.

Cool plants. I have some succulents on mine, and they're arranged randomly to add a touch of nature to the shelves.

Fairy lights. I'll never stop talking about how much I love the twinkle of my fairy lights. They really warm up my shelves.

My record player. It gets a prime spot on my bookshelf.

Scent diffuser. I always have one of these on a shelf: a glass jar with scented oil and reed sticks to help set the mood in my home.

A FUNNY STORY:
"IT WAS A TOTAL BAKING FAIL!"

I love to cook when I'm hanging out by myself at home. But I'm definitely known for making some (okay, a lot of) mistakes in the kitchen. Even if I make a video showing my viewers how to make something, there's a lot more going on behind the scenes that people don't know. My prime example: I had a terrible experience making macarons. The recipe looked so simple at first, so I started around dinnertime and thought I could make them in an hour or two. Well, that is *not* what ended up happening.

My first problem was that I needed almond flour and I couldn't find any, but the recipes all said you could make your own. No big deal, right? So I bought almonds to grind them up into my own almond flour. But what I didn't realize was that you had to keep going at it with a food processor over and over until the flour was perfectly fine. Then you have to sift it. Then, just when you think its powdery enough to be flour . . . it's not. You have to blend it all over again until it's super-thin.

My second issue was that you have to make the batter *really* slowly and can't add too much of something at once or it will throw off the texture. Then you have to pour the batter onto a baking sheet and tap it out on the counter so there are no bubbles in the batter whatsoever.

Finally, after you put the cookies in the oven, they're supposed to bake so that they have "feet" on the bottom—I don't know if you've ever seen a macaron, but the top half of the macaron is super-smooth and round, while the bottom has a textured surface called "feet," apparently. Well, I couldn't get the feet the first time. I was like, "Why didn't I get the *feet*?!" So I had to make a whole new batch.

When I made the cookies a second time, they *looked* really good, but when I took a bite, they were really hard and I felt like I was going to break my teeth, so I couldn't post that take either.

For my third batch, all the cookies caved in and had holes in them.

So I made a *fourth* batch. They were not perfect, but I was so frustrated, I was like, "I'm just using these ones!" By that time, I had stayed up all night, and I didn't finish filming the results of my final cookies until 10 or 11 am. I'll say it again, guys: 10 or 11 am. Of course, on camera I was like, "Woooo, first try! Took like forty minutes!" But in reality? It was probably around seventeen *hours*.

Now it's much easier to make that kind of cookie because they have macaron-making kits with almond flour and pre-measured ingredients and special trays so you get the feet! I'm proud of myself that I made them from scratch, but I won't make anything that complicated again! The joy I get from cooking and baking doesn't come from how difficult a recipe is; it comes from making something delicious in the kitchen, just for me.

The *Easiest* Cookie: Mini Vegan Choco Chip Cookies

Ever since my macaron-making debacle, I've preferred to stick to uncomplicated cookie recipes. This one is adapted from a Betty Crocker cookie recipe I found. (Thanks, girl!) It's made with simple vegan ingredients that make a perfect batch for a night with Netflix as your own BFF.

INGREDIENTS

⅓ **cup coconut oil**

⅓ **cup packed brown sugar**

⅓ **cup sugar**

1 **tsp vanilla**

¼ **cup almond milk**

1¼ **cups flour**

½ **tsp baking soda**

½ **tsp baking powder**

¼ **tsp salt**

5 **oz of vegan dark chocolate chips**

¼ **cup coconut flakes**

TO MAKE THE COOKIES

Step 1: Preheat oven to 350°F.

Step 2: In a bowl, mix together the coconut oil and both sugars. Then stir in the vanilla and almond milk.

Step 3: Add the flour, baking soda, baking powder, and salt and mix until dough forms. Then stir in the chocolate chips and coconut flakes.

Step 4: Roll tiny balls the size of a teaspoon and place them onto an ungreased cookie sheet, with about an inch between each for spreading.

Step 5: Bake seven-to-eight minutes, or until the tiny edges turn light brown. Remove from the oven and let cool, before popping a hot melty one into your mouth!

MY 5 FAVORITE BOOKS

Nearly every book I am reading these days is a self-help book. (I suppose if my bookshelf could speak, it would probably say something like, "Um, Bethany, is everything okay out there? I'm a little worried!") It's my thing. I love diving into my psyche and learning about myself so I can become the best me. Here are my favorites right now:

- *The Power of Now* by Eckhart Tolle
- *The Mastery of Self* by Don Miguel Ruiz
- *Shantaram* by Gregory David Roberts
- *The Motivation Manifesto* by Brendon Burchard
- *The Four Agreements* by Don Miguel Ruiz

I'm Obsessed With . . . My Record Player

I love my record player. There's something so nostalgic about it; it feels like a trip back in time—as in, back to before I was even born! There's also something beautiful about the act of pulling out a record and setting it up, as opposed to just "tap tap tap" on Spotify. The atmospheric quality that a record player adds to a room is incomparable.

I normally keep my two most-played records on the shelf, and store the rest in my office. Other than the current albums I'm loving, I also have a huge collection of Christmas records: *How the Grinch Stole Christmas, A Christmas Story, A Charlie Brown Christmas*, and so many more!

Bedroom Inspo:
What I Love About My Bedroom

I try to go to bed every night around 10 or 11 pm so I can be up at 6 or 7 am. That way, I'm on my game, more energized, and more productive throughout the day. And to get a good night's sleep, I have a great bed. I love relaxing on it with my laptop, and I've decorated it to feel like I'm in a hotel.

- The headboard is really important to me. It's like the centerpiece of the room. Mine is a white, tufted one that feels elegant and cozy.

- My duvet and bedding are all white—hotel style—with about six white pillows.

- I have a memory foam topper under my sheets that molds to your body and feels amazing.

- I layer a lot of blankets when I sleep. One of them is a yellow crocheted blanket my grandma made that I'll reach for at night.

- For a pop of color, I sometimes lay a light blue-and-white duvet on top of my bed.

- My bedroom walls have a light blue accent color that is really soothing.

- No TV. I took mine out so I would be more encouraged to read and sleep, rather than binge-watch *OITNB*.

How I... Plan a Dinner Party

I love being home alone, but there's also something so special about inviting people over and sharing your personal space. One of my favorite ways to invite people over is by having a dinner party.

Growing up, I had dinner with my family every night. So now, making a big meal for my friends helps create a family-like feeling among us. My favorite way to feed them is with a backyard dinner party that's beautiful, chill, and fun. Whether you invite two people or ten, you can still make it an event.

Location: I love how Zen and peaceful it feels to eat dinner outside—I recommend it, if you can. It makes decorating even more fun because you can work nature into your decor.

Lighting: I like to play up the nature fantasy by putting lanterns in the trees or in the bushes by the table. You can also hang a string of bulb lights along the back of your house to light up your table using extension cords plugged into an outdoor outlet, or one snuck through an open window closest to your table.

Tablecloth: Cover a real or makeshift table in brightly colored or tribal fabric to really make it pop.

Table decor: Put baby succulents in glass containers or pots on the table, keeping with the nature scene. Or line up Mason jars along the center length of the table with a brightly colored flower bloom in each one. I also like to decorate the table with candles and food we can nibble on while we catch up before the main course.

Place settings: Use glassware in bright colors that make the table even more festive. And be sure to use cloth napkins, real plates, and your nicest flatware to make it feel special. You can also write a simple name card for each guest, in nice writing, on thick cardstock.

Menu: I love dishes full of bright, light, healthful vegetables. My favorite meal combo: cauliflower tacos, roasted asparagus, and cilantro lime rice, with a watermelon drink to wash it down. (See recipes on next pages.)

Cauliflower Tacos with Purple Slaw and Avocado Cream

CAULIFLOWER TACOS

INGREDIENTS

- ½ **head cauliflower, chopped into florets** (makes three tacos)
- 2 **tbsp olive oil**
- 1 **tsp chili powder**
- **salt and pepper, to taste**
- **package of corn tortillas**
- **cilantro, to taste**

TO MAKE THE CAULIFLOWER TACOS

Step 1: Preheat oven to 425°F.

Step 2: Cut cauliflower into bite-sized florets. Toss them in a bowl with olive oil, chili powder, and a sprinkle of salt and pepper, then lay on a baking sheet.

Step 3: Roast for fifteen to twenty minutes, until parts of the cauliflower are browning, but tender.

Step 4: Place a spoonful of roasted cauliflower on a corn tortilla, and top with slaw, avocado cream, and cilantro to garnish.

PURPLE CABBAGE SLAW

INGREDIENTS

- 2 **cups purple cabbage**
- ¼ **cup fresh lime juice**
- 1 **tbsp apple cider vinegar**
- ½ **tbsp agave**
- **salt and pepper, to taste**

TO MAKE THE SLAW

Step 1: Shred the cabbage or slice it as thinly as possible into ribbons.

Step 2: In a separate bowl, combine the lime juice, vinegar, agave, salt and pepper and mix thoroughly.

Step 3: Pour juice over the cabbage and toss together.

AVOCADO CREAM

INGREDIENTS

- 1 **avocado**
- ¼ **cup lime juice**
- 1 **tsp cumin**
- **salt**

TO MAKE THE AVOCADO CREAM

Blend the avocado, lime juice, cumin, and salt into a creamy consistency that you can spoon onto tacos.

Roasted Asparagus

INGREDIENTS

4 to 6 stalks of asparagus per person
1 tbsp olive oil
salt and pepper, to taste
½ cup lemon juice

TO MAKE THE ASPARAGUS

Step 1: Preheat the oven to 425°F.

Step 2: Clean the asparagus and remove the inedible bases of the stems. (Hold both ends of one piece of asparagus, and bend the bottom half until part of the base snaps off on its own. Cut the other stalks of the asparagus in the same spot, and discard the ends.)

Step 3: Toss the cut asparagus in olive oil, lay on a baking sheet, and sprinkle with salt and pepper.

Step 4: Roast for about fifteen minutes, just until the asparagus heads begin to brown and the stalks are still bright green but tender.

Step 5: Remove from oven and squeeze fresh lemon juice on top before serving.

Cilantro Lime Rice

INGREDIENTS

1 tbsp grape seed oil

½ large onion, finely chopped

2 cups long white rice

3 to 4 cups veggie broth

zest of 2 well-washed, organic limes

juice of 3 limes

head of cilantro, chopped well

salt, to taste

TO MAKE THE RICE

Step 1: Sauté the onion in the oil over medium heat for about five minutes, until soft.

Step 2: Add the rice and salt and cook, stirring constantly, for about three minutes to lightly cook the rice.

Step 3: Add 2 cups of the vegetable broth, the zest, and only ⅔ of the lime juice, then bring to a boil.

Step 4: Simmer for twenty minutes, continuing to add broth as needed while rice is cooking, to keep it from sticking or drying out.

Step 5: Remove from heat, and pour in the final juice of one lime and the fresh cilantro and toss.

Watermelon Freshie

INGREDIENTS
watermelon (1½ cups of cut melon per person)
lime

TO MAKE THE FRESHIE
Cut up the watermelon and toss it in a blender or NutriBullet. Blend it into liquid and pour into a glass. Squeeze a large wedge of lime into the drink and serve.

DIY Party Game for Great Conversation

I have friends who do dinner parties at their house and always invite new people. To make sure that everyone participates in the conversation, the host will kick off the dinner by going around the table and having everyone answer the same question: "What was the high point of your week, and the low point of your week?" I didn't know about seventy percent of the people there the first time I attended one of these parties, so this was a perfect way to encourage good conversation around the table. I think it would be even more fun to present this as a game so the questions might feel less scary or intimidating, and even friends who know each other well might learn a few things.

WHAT YOU'LL NEED

Paper, scissors, a marker, and a bowl.

HOW TO MAKE IT

Step 1: Cut paper into squares and write a deep question on each piece of paper. Write at least as many questions as there are people.

Step 2: Fold up the questions and put them in the bowl.

Step 3: At some point between courses, pass the bowl so that everyone gets to pick and answer one fun question.

Here are some of my favorite questions:

- "What's been scaring you most recently?"
- "What's been holding you back recently?"
- "If your wish could come true tonight, what would it be?"
- "What's the last thing that bummed you out?"
- "What are you looking forward to this month?"
- "What did you learn today?"
- "What are you most grateful for right now?"

Life Is Your Party

The way I see it, each of our lives is like one big party. Every day is something to celebrate. And as the hosts of our own "life" gatherings, we get to plan our themes, decorate with our vibes, and choose the songs that make us want to get up and dance. But most of all, it means we can invite only the people we want around us to our life party—those who love us, support us, challenge us, and help make our life experience the best it can possibly be.

You've seen what my life party looks like. What does *yours* look like? Who's on your guest list and what's on your playlist? Make your mind up and get your party going. Life's too short not to celebrate today.

Thank you!

I'm so happy you joined me, and I hope you had as much fun reading my stories as I did writing them.

My wish is that some of my ideas or experiences might inspire you. Maybe in little ways, sparking some creative ideas each time you make those small decisions about what to eat or wear or make. But I hope they also inspire you in a larger way, to take care of your body and your mind, and to reach for what *you* want to achieve. And if you get scared, remember this:

Before I was on YouTube, I was shy and never lived life to the fullest. I had to face and overcome fear after fear to get to where I am today. And this book in your hands was *one* of those fears, just another thing I was too scared to even try. But I did it! And I'm proud of myself for that. So I hope you will think of it as a sign that you can do anything, and that you will accomplish great things. I promise.

I don't know if you ever feel like I did, but I used to worry so much about fitting in—in school, with friends, with other people's expectations of me. Now, I find more power in *un*-fitting-in. I see "different" as a positive characteristic—and embracing your difference and sharing your talents with the world may be the first step to becoming who you're supposed to be. Life has so many amazing things to offer. I hope you reach for it all—and I hope you do it all *your* way.

Be happy. Work hard. Be kind. Stay strong. And appreciate every moment.

xo,

Bethany

Acknowledgments

There are so many people who have helped me with this book, as well as my career that brought me to this book, and I'd like to express my gratitude to them all.

First, my team who is always there for me. To Jon Moonves for handling all the stuff I don't want to (which is a *lot* of stuff). He's been working with me since I was an awkward teenager, helping guide me above and beyond the job. To Jen Abel for putting up with me—especially all the times I ignore her phone calls because I don't want to hear what she's going to tell me. I rely on her for so much. To Jon Teiber for your guidance and for being a perfect subject in all the random Snapchat filters I've used on him without him knowing.

I also want to thank everyone involved in bringing this book to life. To my amazing editors Jeremie Ruby-Strauss and Nina Cordes for believing in the project and devoting so much to it, making it the best it can possibly be. To Jaime Putorti and Jason Snyder for the beautiful design. To Cait Hoyt for making the magic happen from the start. To Amy Spencer for always having incredible energy, eating acai bowls with me, and helping me with a project that is so incredibly close to my heart. You are truly inspiring, and I'm beyond happy to call you a friend. To Sky Gaven for helping my creative vision come to life visually, and for always bringing me coffee when she knows I need it. And to Kip Zachary and Courtney Nanson, for making me look amazing on days that I only got three hours of sleep before a day I knew I had a shoot . . . but went to bed late anyway. And thank you to all the incredible artists who contributed their talents to my book: Donald Mota, Nancy "Uninanti" Ventura, Alonso "Zoe" Barbosa, Erik Avellaneda, Hector Toro, Jhonatan "Maya" Hernandez, Rebecca "Kalypso" Gonzales, Brooke Marie Reiser, Emma Feil, and AnnMarie Hoang.

Also at Simon & Schuster, thank you to Louise Burke, Jen Bergstrom, Jen Robinson, Liz Psaltis, John Vairo, Lisa Litwack, and Stephanie DeLuca for all your hard work.

I'd like to thank my friends for always being there, for teaching me more than I ever knew, and for reminding me not to stress out so much and enjoy life a little more.

The biggest thank-you goes to my family, who has been there since day one—uh, literally! To my dad for being not just my dad, but also my manager who has supported all of my crazy ideas and helped get me where I am

today. To my mom for not freaking out when I said I wanted to start posting videos of myself on the Internet (can you imagine?) and for being so incredibly supportive of me in every way. And to my sister, Brittany, for listening to me when I went on for hours about my boy problems, and for giving me my niece, Marin, who I get to dress up and hand back to you when she gets a little too loud.

And finally, I want to say thank you to you. Thank you for sharing in this book with me (and reading it all the way to here!). And to those of you who are also my viewers and followers, thank you for sticking with me through all of my weird phases and horrible fashion choices, and being a part of my family online. You guys truly inspire me every day.

Photo Credits

Interior photographs, except where noted, by Sky Gaven.

Photo by Emma Feil Photography, pages vi and 29.

Courtesy of Tony Mota, page xviii.

Courtesy of Tammy Mota, pages xx–xxi.

Courtesy of Bethany Mota, page 19.

Photo by Jhonatan "Maya" Hernandez, page 68.

Wardrobe Credits

DIY By Panida, Amarilo, Vida Kush, Missguided, Gold Hawk, Grlfrnd Denim, Sol Sana, Front Row Shop, Jessica Alba x DL1961, Stuart Weitzman, The Jetset Diaries.